As I Saw It in the Trenches

AUG 2015

As I Saw It in the Trenches

Memoir of a Doughboy in World War I

DAE HINSON

McFarland & Company, Inc., Publishers
Jefferson, North Carolina

Frontispiece: Dae Hinson, ca. 1930

LIBRARY OF CONGRESS CATALOGUING-IN-PUBLICATION DATA

Hinson, Dae.
   As I saw it in the trenches : memoir of a doughboy in
World War I / Dae Hinson.
     p.   cm.
   Includes bibliographical references and index.

   ISBN 978-0-7864-9873-4 (softcover : acid free paper) ∞
   ISBN 978-1-4766-2002-2 (ebook)

   1. Hinson, Dae—Diaries.   2. World War, 1914–1918—
Campaigns—France.   3. Louisiana. National Guard. Infantry
Regiment, 156th—Biography.   4. Soldiers—United States—
Diaries.   5. United States. Army—Biography.   6. World War,
1914–1918—Personal narratives, American.   I. Title.
II. Title: Memoir of a doughboy in World War I.

D548.H55 2015
940.4'1273092—dc23
[B]   2015011400

BRITISH LIBRARY CATALOGUING DATA ARE AVAILABLE

On the cover: "Over the top"—American soldiers answering
the bugle call to "charge," March 25, 1918 (Library of Congress)

Printed in the United States of America

McFarland & Company, Inc., Publishers
 Box 611, Jefferson, North Carolina 28640
  www.mcfarlandpub.com

Acknowledgments

After trying for several months to get someone's attention in regard to my uncle's memoir, my dear friend, Dr. Jack Guerry, said to me, "Why don't you call the Louisiana State Archives?" I did, and talked to Dr. Florent Hardy. I would like to thank Dr. Hardy for his constant enthusiastic spirit regarding this memoir. He has been so encouraging in his belief in the memoir's value. It was wonderful to get a copy into the Louisiana Archives because my uncle was from Louisiana. Dr. Hardy immediately had hopes for this memoir either in print or film. People should have the opportunity to read the memoir. I believe it is as timely now as it was when it was written. Thank you, Dr. Hardy, for your encouragement. I also would like to thank Joan West for taking the original copy and putting it on the computer. This took hours of careful work because the copy my uncle had typed in 1933 was very dim and Joan achieved an exact copy of my uncle's words. She was incredibly caring in the work. She, too, thought my uncle's memoir was important and encouraged me to try to get it published. I also would like to thank Ellen Chang Vaughan, my friend and former student, for some last details of work with the computer to get this into good form for publishing. This project was very important to me. It could not have been completed without the help of these wonderful people.

My uncle never spoke of his experiences in World War I. I knew him for 48 years. He had trouble swallowing because he had been gassed in the War. As I read his memoir, I realized my uncle could write in an important human and compelling way. I thought other people should have the opportunity to read about his experience as a soldier in the United States Army during World War I.

—Monte Hill Alexander

October, 1933
Start, LA

You who read this may well count yourselves among the lucky ones; and, also, trusted ones.

A period of more than three years was covered in writing this real war experience of mine, "As I Saw It in the Trenches." It took much effort and time.

"As I Saw It in the Trenches" is held most sacred by myself. Anyone can easily incur my wrath by misplacing or losing one, just one, page of it, as this would completely disconnect the wording of the original.

This is only the "original," but I fathom it as much as the story in the revised and completed form.

The author
Solomon D. Hinson
Start, LA

Table of Contents

1

Introduction

"As I Saw It in the Trenches"

It is on April 7, 1917 that I travel from my home in the direction of DeRidder, Louisiana. Meeting a friend in the road, he says, "You are in for it. The United States has declared war upon Germany."

I presume he thinks I am anxious to join the army or some other branch of the service preparatory to entering the struggle in Europe. However, I have not one time anticipated joining any branch of war service in the event our country did go to war.

Now that the United States has declared war upon the German Empire, and that men will more than likely be conscripted into the service, I shall feel embarrassed should I fail to be among the first to go to the training camp.

As time lingers on, Congress passes a bill authorizing men to be conscripted into service. Most of the community friends seem to think I will be among the first to enter the camp. It must just be a vague idea they possess for I do not see wherein I am more liable to be first than anyone else. However, I, myself, have a like premonition; and while I do not insinuate to my folks that I am anxious to be among the selects, I do go so far as to ask the parish officials my possibility of being in the first group to leave for camp. Assuring me of a splendid chance, I rest quite at ease until the names first appear on the list on the court house front at Leesville.

Naturally my folks, especially my mother and father, are reluctant to see me go away to war. This worries me considerably, but worrying that I might have to go I think it much better to feel as I do about going away.

As I Saw It in the Trenches

(In the following paragraph, the first words of each line are missing because the script became illegible after the passing of time.)

that the names of the first conscripts will be
e September 1, my father and I go to town to see
e list. We both look over the list and see to my deep
my name posted. I am sure my father can easily
re of attitude that I am sorely disappointed.
g to me that I seek seclusion for awhile in
fy myself against grief of not being able to
ing out on the streets, one of my friends
ws leaving? "Leaving for training camp
replies. "I suppose they will be leaving
self, I guess I will wait a good while
ne is posted," he says. "Being so convincing
d re-examine the list whereupon I
he top. Now, I return home to await
or getting off to train
hardly
ates seems very much awake to the danger
and future   atens it over there.

The Draft Act being enacted by Congress, training quarters are being constructed by almost unbelievable rapidity in various sections of the country. Only a few months after declaring war, conscripts and volunteers are being rushed to the training camps to be drilled and trained by experienced officers.

It is now September 17, 1917. The first conscripts have assembled at Leesville preparatory to being transferred to Camp Pike, Arkansas. There is not as much smiling and back-slapping as one usually sees in the town. Contrarily, there is more solemnity than anyone has ever witnessed previously. As for myself, I have no direct dependents and as a result I feel quite at ease in that one respect. On the other hand, there are several men who have wives, however, and naturally carry a strong reluctance to leaving them. Hence, you can account for the downhearted attitude that prevails among the men and their families.

The townspeople are extremely courteous to we boys; showing us respect by carrying us car-riding and assuring us of deep sympathy while away in the war.

While waiting for the train, there is much affectionate embracing that takes place. Some of the boys acknowledge their reluctance to leaving by breaking down and weeping. Inwardly I am much touched; but outwardly I think I display a considerably pleasant attitude until my father chokingly asks that I always be a good boy while away.

The trip to camp is quite lively, as all boys seem to have lost conscience of their grief and have taken up the bright side of life. Everyone to a man seems full of life; and demonstrates it by yelling and screaming while passing through towns. One comical fellow amuses everybody in the car he occupies by asking people at the different stops when the 2:30 train went through.

We are now at Camp Pike. Everything seems much opposite to what I thought it would. I am somewhat surprised at the courtesy shown us on reaching the camp. I suppose they do not care to make us too homesick through being too positive and cross.

A few days pass before being issued uniforms. We only drill an hour or two a day. Everybody believing he would find himself in a new uniform soon after reaching camp, carried only the civilian clothes he had on his person. Therefore, drilling in our suits causes them to become extremely soiled in a short time.

A few days later we find ourselves in new khaki clothes. Nearly every one of us presents a slouchy, awkward appearance, the chief cause being due to our not knowing how to adjust our differently-made clothing to fit our persons; then also we do not, of course, move about with the snap and agility of trained men.

As time rocks along, we become more accustomed to camp life, our clothing, food, and drill. Some of the men kick about what they have to eat. However, I think this is a natural trait of theirs and it is quite probable they are relishing more good food here than they were getting at home.

I think that which makes camp life so disagreeable to the soldiers at first is the many limited privileges they are used to having as civilians. The sedations, principally due to quarantines resulting from epidemics, are aggravating to most of us. All drill and no amusement goes hard with the newly-conscripted men and generally results in many of the men participating in games of chance; taking absence without leave; or violating the army rules in other ways.

As I Saw It in the Trenches

If various forms of athletics, such as track, tennis, baseball, basketball, etc., were encouraged more, it would go far in relieving us of our civilian memories. Constant shift of mind is the best cure for my homesick blues; and it undoubtedly serves equally as well for others. The best cure for everyone, I notice, is a good long walk out into the country on Sunday afternoons. Yes, indeed, any boy and his buddy, more than anything else, enjoys lying on a quiet hillside far removed from the sight of soldiers and camp, conversing leisurely of the past but not the probable future. For reflecting the mind over the hill to the future, and across the ocean to the long, drawn-out horrors, a sinking unhappiness strolls lazily through the bodily anatomy, due to our enemy generally carrying the reins of victory in his hand. The news from abroad causes it to seem too certain that we will have to go over there and pit our facial exposures at the fate of the bayonets, machine-guns, poisonous gasses and tormenting shellfire we are so lectured about in camp.

The captain, I think, is none too reticent in telling those of us in his Company of the horrors and fatalities we are nearly sure to meet with over there. He especially shakes us in expressing his belief that many, if not all of us, will be resting under the sods of France within less than a year's time. His motive, after all, might be sound in that it is certain to excite in us the realism of a serious episode, thereby causing us to get down to brass tacks in preparing to meet the crisis that might, in the near future, determine our individual fate.

I, myself, am already becoming awakened to the fact that my past has been a sleepy one. It was never hard for me to understand that a healthy physique was extremely important for one's welfare. On the other hand, I had too seldom encountered difficulties that convincingly demonstrated to me the advantages of a trained and educated mind. The reader is correct in concluding that my education, at the time I am supposed to be writing, is limited, and hence, is a big handicap to me during my time in service.

Now it is that I can do nothing other than accept that for which I am best suited, be it a "buck private" in the rear ranks, a flunky in the kitchen, or a fireman on an incinerator. But I never relished the idea of being a flunky; hence, I intend to put in some time practicing different drills in order to make a good soldier in the ranks.

2

Getting Accustomed
to Camp Life

There are few things more fascinating to watch than a company of well-trained soldiers drilling. In fact, there are other things that appeal to me but little less. The chance of building up a splendid physique is great. One can always get a wrestling or boxing match. He can take it upon himself to do many forms of athletics not encouraged in camp. This very few ever do, however.

The requirements that all men must shave, bathe and present clean appearances most assuredly is a blessing to many an individual, and the snappy pace he acquires as a soldier is sure to send home an entirely different man.

A few months in Camp have passed now. Most everyone seems to have taken on a different attitude of life. We realize more fully that we are not off on just a pleasure trip. On the other hand, we realize we must make haste and win the war, lest Germany and her few allies will. Not only that but our uniforms are not so slouchy and baggy-fitting about the knees and seat as was the case at first. The blouse does not fit so loosely about the waist and hips now. And with very few exceptions, we present quite a soldiery appearance.

Camp Pike is a very delightful training camp. The low range of mountains on which the camp is situated is remarkably pretty. The hazy horizons to be viewed from camp are invitingly picturesque. The surrounding atmosphere itself is a tonic, making the camp rather a health resort. The accommodations here are far ahead of those of other camps, we are told. The bath houses and personal accommodations are generally conveniently located. So, therefore, before this war is over, we might wish we had stayed in Camp Pike the entire time.

Every so often, it is mentioned that the Louisiana men will probably be transferred to Camp Beauregard, near Alexandria, Louisiana. Most all the men are in favor of being transferred in that they will be more accessible to their homes. But as for myself, I feel reluctant to leaving Camp Pike.

Finally, official reports make it known that we have been assigned to Camp Beauregard and will be leaving for same within a short time. The report makes many a man happy. Several, however, who want to go and cannot due to their having red measles, are very unhappy.

The likelihood of my becoming separated from the good old big-hearted cook, whose name is Ben Jarrell, and who is from my home neighbor, leaves one guessing if I will be as well fed in the future as he has fed me in Camp Pike. Ben and I fraternize a great deal and when no one else knows about it we are in the kitchen partaking of the very best food the army furnishes.

Ben is being transferred to Camp Beauregard too. But we do not know if we will be assigned to the same company or not.

3

Camp Beauregard

Having trained in Camp Pike nearly two months, we are now on our way to Camp Beauregard. Inspection by army physicians reveals that several including myself have measles. This is sad news all right and to add to the sorrow, we are quarantined upon reaching camp. We are quarantined on a lonely knoll about a mile from the main camp. It is a very lonesome place. The next day I try to persuade the doctors to assign me to a Company, but they do not listen to my pleas, however, until they are convinced that I am good and well.

A week passes before the doctors pronounce me well. I am assigned to Co. L, 156 Infantry. The Company is made up chiefly of Louisiana Frenchmen whom I find, as a rule, to be very nice and friendly. It is only a question of time until I am looked upon as one of the old regular men and enjoying the companionship of the soldiers very much.

My good friend Ben is missing. This is a great disappointment indeed. It is a month or more before I locate him. On one Sunday I learn, through meeting one of my old Camp Pike friends, where Ben has been assigned. Looking him up, he gives me a great big feed and assures me that he will be glad to repeat the act every time I call around. He finds me calling around very often from then on.

Camp Beauregard is not nearly so delightful, in most respects, as Camp Pike. First, we have only tents instead of barracks in which to sleep. Second, the low level surface makes it very disagreeable during rainy weather; and third, various epidemics are so frequent that almost incessant quarantines are necessary.

The coming of March closes the curtain on a hard and disagreeable winter. Aside from the hard winter, many of the men of Company L, to say nothing of the camp as a whole, have been suffering from severe cases of pneumonia. About seven of those carried to the hospital were succumbed. I experienced a very severe case of pneumonia myself, and my folks were advised by telegram that the crisis in my case might result in death.

After regaining my strength, I resume drill again, going through eight hours of drill daily. It seems like being back home again. The boys seem to be glad that I am back with the old Company again and as for myself, I am tickled to see all the old boys who I have learned to admire so much. Having been away and now back again, my mind, more than any time previously, is more relieved from home and the pleasant memories back there. In other words, I am more adapted and reconciled to my army environment than ever before.

The bayonet practice, which is a newly introduced drill in the Company during my absence, quickly gains my favor and I take special interest in this phase of training. As for me, there are more thrills and kick in displaying the use of bayonet than any of the various forms of drill. Attacking the dummies, which are made of small branches of trees, thrusting bayonet through them, then almost knocking the support with the butt of the rifle, is fun indeed. The fun here should be made the great of too, for there is sure to be little fun when the real German, himself, is attacked. And if by magic the dummy should thrust forth a long shining bayonet in defiance to our charges, the fun would be finished and curse would, no doubt, rain down upon the head of the cruel inventor of the dreaded weapon.

Captain Frank Mayes, the rather reticent but sincere captain, in his few words warns his men of the difficult tasks awaiting them over yonder, and that thoroughness acquired through concentrative training is the best weapon that one can carry with him to the front. The captain stresses cleanness and care of the body and perfection and agility on the part of the soldier. His visual response to the clean and agile soldier is proof enough that he admires those important qualities in the soldier. Captain Mayes is particular in selecting his non-commissioned officers as he feels that perfection and thoroughness are responsible for the men's lives over there and that these officers are responsible for these important acquisitions. In the event a non-com fails to impress him, he relieves him of his commission and stripes or as it is so commonly expressed in camp, "busts" him. At one time, the captain, through his determination to have capable non-coms or none at all, "busts" about half of them and tries out several privates to determine their capabilities.

It is now early May. Captain Mayes rumors it to the effect that most all the non-coms and all privates will be en route to France pretty soon. He expresses himself as believing that we are able to give the Germans surprising competition. This sounds good, but still, through reading the papers, we feel that the Germans will give us more competition than we care for. In this connection, do not let anyone flatter you into believing that you would like to have a chance to hear the bullets zip close to your person and face an army of well-trained and determined antagonists. Also, do not allow him to lead you to believe he would relish it either.

The morale of the worn-out French and English soldiers in France seems at very low ebb. Of course the morale of the German soldiers is on the incline as a result. In fact, the Germans seem more certain of victory now than in early 1917. The fall of Russia in the latter part of 1917 and the present retreating French and English armies would naturally lead the German army to believe victory is only a question of a few weeks. Now that Russia has already quit the fight as a result of the fall of the government, the German units in that section, known as the Eastern Front, have been transferred to the Western Front preparatory to making a determined drive for Paris. The relief from the Eastern Front is having its effect too, as one can easily gather through reading the papers.

May 1918 finds the German army within thirty miles of Paris. Therefore, it is plain that if the German army is stopped the Americans units must hurry to France and strengthen the Allied forces lest it seems the capitol is doomed to fall into the hands of the enemy. I do not mean to discredit the French and English soldiers when I say what I have. They have fought as nobly as any soldiers that have ever lived.

The middle of May truly brings about a crisis in the case of the Allied forces over there at the present. But yet it is thought and hoped that the Americans will have time to get there in time to reverse the conclusion that Paris will soon fall before the Germans. Camp Beauregard soldiers are being sent over as casualties to replace the men of the depleted companies that are to fight as units. At present there are no American units, to speak of, fighting in the trenches, but it is expected that there will be in the course of a short time. Therefore, we will be assigned to a unit after reaching France.

4

Off to France

It is May the twentieth and now the old men move out preparatory to going over. New conscripts pour into the camp replacing us almost by the time we leave our companies. These new fellows are comical to look at because of their stooped shoulders, long awkward strides and lack of a soldierly appearance. This compared with the trained soldiers who have acquired erect forms, short, snappy steps and health and physiques descriptive of flaming youths. We old men get much fun in taunting them with our boast that we will have the war won before they become acquainted with the command "Squads Right and Squads Left." On the contrary, they make it sort of embarrassing for us when they reply that we have been off to war nearly a year and have not yet fired a gun. Leaving camp May the twenty-fifth, we pull into Toulon, New Jersey on May the thirty-first. In the delightful training camp at this place, we stop over until June the seventh at the end of which time we continue on to Hoboken, New Jersey where we take the boat Manchuria to France. Having contracted a severe cold during my trip to Hoboken, the trip to France is but little pleasant. Besides being ill, the solemn attitude of the men and the possibility of meeting with disaster at the cost of the German submarines add to the unpleasantness of the voyage on the way over.

Coming out on the deck the morning of June 19 reveals that we have anchored in the harbors of an entirely different-looking town to any I have seen in the United States. The houses are generally constructed of stone and are very old-looking. The town viewed from the boat seems very dull and quiet.

About an hour later we leave the boat, I learn the name of the town is St. Nazaire, France. Here, I see the first pair of wooden shoes in my

11

life. The shoes are worn by a young girl who tries to sell nuts. (Missing page 13.)

We do have a little evidence that we will be headed for the front near Chatteau Thierry when we pull out of St. Nazaire. The information comes from a first lieutenant, detached to this front in that it is the strongest German offensive on the front at present. He goes on to say that the Germans are expected to attack any time and that we will be held in reserve to act in defense when they do attack. Lastly, he adds that we will be issued everything necessary or at least everything expected of a trench man, at some point further on in the direction of the front.

5

Off to the Front

Leaving the camp June 25, we load on to boxcars. On one end of the car are the words 8 chevaux and on the other end 40 homme. The former meaning of 8 horses will have the occupancy of one end of the car and the latter 40 men on the other. We arrange ourselves accordingly. The locomotive whistles, then puffs, then puffs and we are off to the front.

The ride is most uncomfortable, as one would expect. Those who have previously had access to far better luxury, gripe and complain babyishly of their newly acquired accommodations. On the other hand, more of us are more reticent and if their thoughts are in correlation with my own, they are thinking that the near future awaits for us, accommodations far tougher and less appreciated than even this old boxcar we are in.

This is indeed a splendid course for a "mama petted" good-for-nothing boy who has never had his hands corned with ordinary labor work.

The coming of darkness screens our eyes to the beautiful hills and country to be seen in daylight. During none of my travels have I enjoyed any more beautiful scenery than that of France.

In the morning, we are halted in a small town. The townsmen seem awfully glad that the Americans are arriving in France and on the way to the front to relieve or reinforce the discouraged French soldiers up there. It is not uncommon at all for these humble peasants to walk up to an American soldier and always gesturing with hands say, "je parle France," which means, "can you speak French?" They frequently are consoled on being answered in French by an American who knows how to speak Cajun, a crude French dialect. Of course, the American Cajun mother tongue is very illiterate French language. However, it seems that, there, the French and Cajun grasp the meaning of enough of each other's words to comprehend the line of thought.

Through interpreting, we who do not understand French, learn from our own soldiers that, up on the front is the next thing to Hell. The French felt that, when a German is shot down, it seems that by miracle another appears, alive, in his place; and that when a Frenchman is killed he stays killed and unfortunately, there seems to be no one to take his place. I gather from all this that they mean there are too plenty Germans.

The chief wish expressed by the French is peace again. It is very easy to discern through their solemnity and actions that they are extremely tired of war. Maybe they would not display such vivid dissatisfaction were the war being decided on the grounds of another country. But knowing that about one-third of their country has already undergone the most complete destruction of any country in history makes them most desirous of peace, possibly, even at the cost of defeat.

While in general, these people are very disgusted, it is fascinating to observe the happiness they display in response to the least impulse. The gift of a cigarette, an American coin, or any valueless article, presented by an American soldier seems to tickle them more than a hundred-dollar gift received by an ordinary American civilian. I think in this case, there is an outstanding mark of differentiating between the rich and the pauper child.

It is found contrary to the statement often expressed back in America that the French are awfully hospitable and eager to show courtesy to the foreigner often at their own expense. They are kindly met all right but so far they have carried no expense with it. But it is very probable that there would be inexpensive courtesy displayed in any country upon whose grounds the most terrible war in history was being fought. And should the soils of the wealthiest country be ground into powder with increased barrages, and its towns smashed and scrambled until not a whole brick remained, it would mean the elimination of so much foolish aristocracy and puny pride, existing among those able to possess modern comforts to say nothing of being really wealthy. Do not interpret me as meaning that war is a good thing to have in a country, however.

5. *Off to the Front*

Here, I witness my first destructive ravages caused by bombs. A few weeks previous this town had been bombarded by aeroplanes. The bombs caused little damage other than smashing a large building close by the depot. The building was being used as a warehouse for storing war supplies. It is now that I am convinced of the possible danger and destruction in these bombs we are to encounter at the front.

Three hours after arriving in this town, we leave it, hiking about ten miles and then loading onto trucks, as many as can get on. The ride is rough and very uncomfortable. But after all it is more pleasant than hiking.

The end of our transfer finds us in another small town where it is officially announced we will remain a few days. The town is picturesquely located, being situated between a river and a mountain. The river near the bridge which we cross is much in demand for people wishing to bathe and swim. And we Americans, who do not ever, publicly, witness such scenes back home, suffer shocks of our modesties on seeing a large crowd of men in bathing with nothing on but their birth robes. We would not think so much about it were not the bathing center in plain view of the bridge and nearby dwellings. But it matters not who looks on; for such I understand, is the custom with the French people. Another thing that is humiliating to us is that these countrymen will not seek concealment in response to a natural necessity.

After being assigned to our compartments, which in my and most other cases are those of hay barns, we get on the hunt for the kitchen and water well. The barns are completely void of openings for light and it is necessary that we remove a few shingles from the roof above our pallets in order to have access to light and fresh air. A little exercise in making a bed of the hay and blanket results in a very comfortable bed on which to sleep. In order to subdue the dust, we sprinkle water over the floor and hay two or three times a day.

The kitchen happens to be located just in front of the barn I am in and it takes but a few seconds to get there when the sound for chow is given. While eating, we unimportant privates and non-coms become sorely vexed when a Frenchman, during nearly every meal, fetches out a demijohn of wine and treats the two first lieutenants each to a large glass full of it.

The two lieutenants are the only commissioned officers with us. They will accompany us as far as the front where they will leave us definitely assigned to a Company. They will then return to some seaport in France to bring up the replacement troops. Replacement troops are held in reserve to fill up companies that have become depleted in action on the firing lines.

There is not much here to while away the time with other than a little drill every day, and walking around the town and out a little way into the country. Having no money to spend for any of our cravings, we resort to the next most pleasant pastime which is visiting pear and plum orchards after dark, helping ourselves to the best fruit available. On one occasion, but in the daytime as it happens, a hard-boiled woman catches another boy and me in a plum tree just as we finish filling our blouses with its contents. And while neither of us comprehends a word she says, both of us agree that she uttered not one word of kindness. Her hostile actions had great bearing on our visiting the orchard altogether dark from then on. We both got away all right with our plans.

It is now June 26, 1918. We are issued rifle, cartridge belt and cartridges, helmet and hob-nail shoes. Then we are called to assembly and receive orders to be ready to leave sometime during the morning. While the officers tell us that we are heading for the front, the fact that we are issued firing line equipment is plenty indicative to let us know that the firing line is our destination. Now this business of moving about all the time is fast becoming a monotony with me as I always had a horror for such. But my likes and dislikes have no weight in adjusting same. Then should I be rewarded with a piece of cake and glass of sweet milk in response to all of my dislikes, there would doubtless be nothing but dislikes in my plasma thereby resulting in my disapproval of the best can of corned beef in France.

6

Our Assignment

We are again transferred by means of trucks. At the end of the ride, we unload in a forest. Here we are instructed not to unroll pack and at night never to strike matches for fear that the enemy might spot us and begin shelling. This is enough to convince us that we are close to the front and that it is meant that we will face the Germans in their next on-to-Paris offensive. The forest is ragged and torn from the effects of shellfire. The explosive and withered leaves create a peculiar odor and such that causes several to complain of dizziness and headaches.

During the last few hours of which time we have been huddled here in this seeming God forsaken territory, I am stimulated with feeling and assurance that I, as well as many others, have opened a door to the visions of a far different confronting than any previously confronted. Tomorrow, or at least the near future, holds in its hands the decision of our destinies. The thoughts of the good old civilian privileges, as crude as some of them have been, are gloriously appreciated. How sweet it would be if it were possible, here, to turn back and live it all over again. Still it is folly to recall all these sweet recollections. I should think it best to try to forget them as completely as possible and instead train the mind to the effect that it all will be made the best of; whatever the outcome may be.

Before being distributed to our assignments in reserve, we are given a few specific instructions as to what to do while attacking, while being attacked, and while being exposed to gas and shellfire. All the instructions seem very sound and sensible and if executed will no doubt spare the life of many a man. While attacking and being attacked, we are instructed to, at all times, keep the mind operating as smoothly as possible and to keep the body concealed from the enemy as much as possible not to become too inactive.

About ten o'clock, the men are distributed to various sections of the near-by-front reserve. Fifty men including myself take off afoot in the direction of our assignment. Coming to top of a high hill, a flash, resembling lightning, presents itself in the far distance. A few seconds later something is heard squealing in the air high above our heads passing on into the darkness to our rear. Again the flash is seen and the ghostly airman repeats himself.

About a mile further on, we are confronted with the steepest hill I ever saw, or at least the steepest one I ever tried to ascend afoot. It seems more like a mountain than a hill. It is about a half mile from its foot to its crest.

Continuing the hike, we are confronted with the steepest hill I ever tried to ascend afoot. Our packs add to the strain of climbing. Several times we are forced to take on renewed energy through resting. My legs never before trudged under such prolonged strain; and reasoning from the complaints of some of my companions, they are undergoing similar experiences. A tall fellow whose name is Allen, takes the prize for complaints and especially emphasizes that it is ridiculous that a human should be called upon to go through with such brutal agony. He is very reiterative with respect to this one objection but finally becomes somewhat discouraged on being told that he is in the infancy of the hardships and troubles that the near future will pay him off with.

Allen is not a "mama" spoiled baby by any means. He is just a natural born griper and cannot help responding to this characteristic.

The top of the hill being reached, we proceed a little way into a forest where we are told to unroll pack and remain for the night. The next instruction is to "dig in" to which we feel reluctant being so extremely tired after having climbed such a steep hill. But on being informed that we might be introduced to shellfire any time, it becomes quite logical that it might be the best thing to do after all.

So far I, of course, have never seen a small burst and really only have an imagination as to what one looks like. But having seen the effects of bombardments back in the forest, no one need tell me they carry death in their pockets. And from that I have been told about machine guns, it seems that they carry a striking similarity to a mowing machine in a hay field when a group of men get in front of the gun.

6. Our Assignment

Morning. We learn that we have been assigned to Co. M. 3rd. Div. 38th Inf. The captain of the Company informs us of our assignment and assures us that he will do everything possible for our protection; but while in doing this, we must remember to respond to orders and commands promptly. The captain also instructs us as to how to behave while at the mercy of shellfire and machine guns. He impresses me as being a man well capable of commanding a Company of soldiers while in battle. He also impresses me as being a man who will deal kindly with his men if they will permit it. As a matter of fact, I think all the officers and non-commissioned officers as a whole are well selected; and officers who will do their bit in helping win this war for our country. I might be wrong about all of this.

I notice it is now that so many of the good old civilian memories are becoming less frequently spoken of. The conversations that generally involved sweethearts, dances, wild life, and so forth are fast becoming eliminated to be substituted by the one and only one conversation: "WAR." No indeed, a soldier rarely speaks of such, and when he does, he usually rubs his forehead expressing dissatisfaction of the future with a scowling frown and says "Well, I guess it will turn out all right maybe."

7
Constructing Dugouts
and Trenches

It is now July 2, 1918. We find that we will not be altogether idle even though we are not fighting right now. A part of the men are detailed to dig trenches at night and the other part of the men are detailed to construct dugouts during the daytime. The object of digging trenches at night is to shield ourselves from German observation. Of course, it is all right to construct dugouts during the daytime as we are shielded from the enemy aeroplanes and observation balloons by trees and bushes. And, of course, this would be all right in digging trenches too in case they were being dug in a forest. But, as it happens, we are digging our reserve trenches in a large wheat field which necessitates our digging them at night.

Now for the convenience of those who do not understand the meaning of a dugout or what it looks like, I shall attempt to describe same. A hole, nearly always square, and about five feet deep is made in the ground and generally under trees. To protect the men occupying it during shelling, logs are cut and placed side by side all the way across the dugout, then reinforced by another layer laid crosswise the first. Then the rock and dirt made accessible in excavating the dugout is used in covering the logs. The larger rocks are used as the outer covering as they serve well in causing the shell to explode before forcing itself into the interior of the covering or shell hole. The entrance and exit of the dugout are used for each purpose and always opposite the direction of the enemy, as one would naturally expect. This type of dugout is known as the shellproof dugout. The small uncovered type of dugout is known to serve as protection from bullets and spreading shrapnel. Practically no fighting is ever carried on from the shellproof dugout. Its main purpose is to protect men from shell fire during a barrage.

Asking someone just what the meaning of shell fire was, he replied "it is the next thing to hell fire." I do not doubt but that he knows wherein he speaks as he has seen a little service on the front before.

8

First Bombardment

We have lingered along here from day to day constructing dugouts and digging trenches until now it is July 14. I am detailed to dig trenches tonight, and sure enough I act as detailed. By midnight, the trench I dig in reaches a depth of about two feet. Suddenly, it seems that all the war Gods have lighted their torches and declared war upon the universe. The Germans are reporting with an extremely heavy barrage preparatory to launching a determined drive for Paris. The command to lie down in trenches is given. Shells can be heard coming with roaring thunder through the air. They fall all around with the crashing claps of a thousand bolts of lightning. I feel for one of these deadly reports to blow me into bits. Screams are heard close by which is proof enough that some or more have been badly wounded. Some of the bombs fall so close by that they shake me considerably and throw dirt and debris spattering all over me. One shell lights so close that I feel if it repeats itself I will open the door to eternity. It repeats itself and as I hear it come tearing through the air, I hug old mother earth more affectionately than I ever hugged anything before. These shells falling so close to me almost have my name written correctly.

Down the trench a little way I hear some hollers "I am hit." Then he takes to his feet and runs hysterically into the dark uttering words of agony. He has company in that others are wounded, for I hear several screams that evidence the fact that shells are dropping into the trench in several places.

The guns on our side are hurling shells back at the Germans with stubborn resentment. Yes, our men stand by their guns operating them in the middle of biting Hell, in order that the Germans' attempt to cross the Marne River at daylight in the morning will be mocked.

8. First Bombardment

It is dark and I can see nothing but sparks from bursting shells and flashes from our cannon. But I hear aplenty. The noise is so much as to almost lead one to wonder if Germany is falling down upon us. Again and again shells howl through the air, a few seconds later to pour down upon our immediate surroundings, and sometimes upon some of my Company, mixing them with the sods of the Marne in the form of mangled flesh.

Undoubtedly, the wheat will be husked by means of the terrible barrage. The air must hold a great amount of the straw. My shell comes howling through again. Every muscle in my body contracts in response to my fear and heavy suspense that awaits the decision of the determined, vociferous monster. It lands so nearby that I am kind of inclined to ask myself whether or not it hit me.

Again dirt rains down upon me; after which I treat my whole body to a temporary rest through relaxation of my muscles. I am right now undergoing a series of nervous tensions. It seems impossible that I will be able to control my nerves through much more of this. Should they go to pieces, I will suffer what is called "shell shock." I feel like moving from where I am. But why should I, one place being as safe as another, not meaning that any place is safe.

Screams are heard not far away. This adds to the realization that we are subjects at the mercy of whatever the enemy would like to deal out to us. It all also adds to the realization that we were all in Heaven in our country and too inexperienced to know it.

A lengthy figure crawls awkwardly among the shaky doughboys as they sit and lie in wait for a shell to grind their atoms into still more separable particles. The crawling figure is none other than that of Captain Woodside. The captain's bravery and courage is not cowered by the deadly threats of the vociferous bombardment. His words are, "Don't be discouraged, men. At daylight we will meet them face to face. They let us show them the other side of the Marne."

The captain's words are forcible, and he means what he says. He really believes the Germans will suffer a sad surprise in meeting defeat at our resistance.

It is compulsory that the captain crawl from man to man because of thundering of shells and guns that render everything else inaudible at any distance.

As I Saw It in the Trenches

One cannot afford to entertain the idea that the Germans will, tomorrow, increase their salient in the direction of Paris with us their slain victims or prisoners. The Germans are confident that within the next day or two they will have sacked Paris. But Captain Woodside fully intends that they will steer around the position his Company occupies or die in the event they try to pass through. The captain continues on amidst a thousand invitations of flirting death. He seems not conscious that death will claim him in the critical hour that possibly determines the possibility of saving Paris from German capture. Judging from sound, there have fallen, already, enough bombs to destroy two or three cities the size of Paris. And they continue to rain down in un-reducing numbers.

Again, screams indicative of someone or more being hit are heard in different directions. It reminds me of the proverb "There will be wailing and gnashing of teeth," the only difference being that there is wailing and gnashing of teeth here. A little to the rear of our trench, guns continue to belch bombs back to the enemy in resistance and defiance to the destructive and stubborn barrage that has long been and is still raining down upon us. It could easily be termed a miracle as to how it is that the artillerymen can live in the middle of a million chances of death.

Daylight approaches but the shelling is yet too heavy for one to dare chance his life in an effort to get to the dugouts upon the hill lest he be blown to pieces. Then suddenly the captain's voice pierces the bang of the bombs. His strong command is "Follow me up the hill. The Germans are coming and we must meet and stop them." He points abruptly at the top of the hill and says "They must not take our supplies and dugouts. We must beat them there." I do not emerge from the trench until the captain finally commands it. I adjust my limbs preparatory to springing from the shallow trench, when he gestures to follow him to the road and up the steep hill. He, with a loud scream to follow, gestures madly the same command. It is then that we spring from the trench in the midst of bursting bombs. A tree standing close to the juncture of the road and trench is a victim of a shell which explodes sending fragments and shrapnel in every direction. One man is killed outright, and we others are scared almost into believing we are hit.

We inexperienced doughboys are at a complete loss as to what action to take in protecting ourselves from these shells now that we are exposed to them above the surface. All we know to do is just follow orders from the captain and lieutenants in the face of such intense excitement. The tear and splatter of the numerous shells result in temporary disorganization of the Company. Some try to flee up the hill to seek safety in the dugouts. The hill is too steep to permit rapid progress and therefore we are forced to push slowly, contrary to our wishes, up the hill on the top of which we might, through God's wishes, find protection from the metallic beast that have for six hours been growling through the air and exploding at our discontent. They rain down upon the road in front of us as much as to say "We are acting in response to the command of Tyrant Kaiser." Men in khaki tumble at their reports giving their lives for democracy, perhaps, but probably not through such realization but through realization that they are fighting just because they are told to and just because they want to get through with it and go back home. At these critical and seeming inescapable moments, he that entertains the thought of ever reaching home again is just one of un-crushable courage. A lightning-like glance upon a few sleepy faces reveals that hope and courage still rest in the hearts of some of them.

A howling demon screaming through the air lights in the road ahead of me. A doughboy, a victim to its prey, rolls fast down the road with stones and clots of dirt. Should the German who tagged this monster sending him in search of prey know just what happened, I can imagine him practicing his victory smile. Two horses still hitched to and lying almost under a supply wagon lie dead from a merciless bomb that sneaked down upon the team sometime during the night. A man lies limply across the wagon seat, dead either from shock or shrapnel. Another shell falls close to my right, jarring me some and spitting fragments of shells and shrapnel squealing and sputtering into the air.

Rain begins to fall slowly and is a great handicap to us in making it up the steep hill. My back hurts; and legs above the knees are terribly worried and hurting and renders frequent rests necessary. But falling bombs cause me to keep moving most all the time. Finally the hill is mastered as its crest is reached by several of us. It seems that a thousand pounds have been removed from my back as the pains begin leaving.

As I Saw It in the Trenches

While trotting in the direction of the dugouts, I hear a shell coming in my direction. The last thing I remember for a few moments is the shell lighting close to my right. On regaining consciousness, it seems that all my joints have been torn apart and the right side of my face stings all over from small particles of dirt and sand that were sent against it by the explosion of the shell. I am jarred from foot to head and in some parts of my body there is no feeling to speak of. I am so certain that I cannot walk that I do not even attempt to gain my footing and it is by the aid of two other men that I do so. On finding that I have no broken limbs, I feel much relieved over the outcome and proceed slowly in the direction of my destination. Never before had I felt worse and it is only because I am victim of the unmerciful enemy that I am inspired to trudge along and try to reach that dugout that might hold in its interior my deliverance from the determined bombs that are tearing everything on the earth's surface into shreds. Large trees lie sprawled and ragged every-where from the effects of the barrage. The shells still rain down all around and men run here and thither from their vociferous explosions. The surrounding and immediate vicinity is not the same as last evening. The shell-torn ground is not that one could have previously imagined. A new fighter cannot help but feel that Germany is the country that will walk off with the laurels.

Such marked change in scenery cannot help but be nothing more than vivid to even such a haggard, scared and shell-jarred soldier as I. My condition and my strength being absorbed by that shell renders it necessary or, to say the least, compulsory that I rest a bit before com-pleting my journey to the dugouts. So it is that I resolve to take a rest by the root of a large beech tree, using its trunk for a rest for my head. With the lapsing of a few moments, many thoughts flicker through my mind; but it is impossible that the thought of a bright and happy future could be amidst all the thoughts that entertain my hazy and inactive mind. It takes the nerve of a stone wall to enable the mind capable of a few moments' concentration in the midst of these roaring and thunder-ing demons that pour down like slushes of rain. Every moment one can-not refrain from the thought that he will be sacked by one of these ghostly squealers that so often announce their approach from the other side of the Marne. Then it is that one can realize the powerfulness of the Great Divine that holds above all the magic sword directing one's destiny in the heat of Hell itself.

During my few loitering moments, a very strange feeling flashes through me. It is the feeling that the fangs of death are snapping at what few chances of living I have left. Followed by these feelings, a voice from above seems to speak telling me, in as many words, that I had best remove at once lest the end is close at hand. With what little strength I have and with the additional inspired by the spiritual voice, I gain my footing as quickly as possible and proceed very failingly toward the dugouts. My feeling is that something more very serious is to take place within a few moments of time. An excited doughboy running towards me yells out, "Is there any use going any further? The Germans are coming and will soon be here." I presume he must have meant to ask me if there were any more men in the organization who had not yet reached the dugouts. He turns very nervously in the direction of the dugouts and runs toward same before I have to answer. I hear a shell scream through the air with mad velocity. It approaches much closer during every tenth of a second becoming more ghostly-like as it approaches. It suddenly swishes down in the treetops above and more suddenly plows into my tree of rest, sending shrapnel and fragments of shell zipping and spluttering in all directions with blood and death seeming to be the purpose of their adventure. The tree, haggard and gnawed by the powerful bomb, tumbles to the ground with unimaginable speed. A voice from an inanimate source had saved my life; and it is now that I take on courage in my physically unfit body that surely must not be meant to rot in France lest the voice would not have played the spiritual role.

Another horrible but attractive incident takes place when an aerial bomb drops upon a wagon drawn by a horse, littering the wagon and killing the horse outright. I remember so well the fragment of the wagon being forced from the midst of the black smoke and dirt sent into the air by the violent explosion of the bomb. The wagon having been blown loose from the horse, the animal almost turns a somersault, then lies groaning and dying from concussion and no doubt fragments and shrapnel of the shell. The enemy plane strutting its large black cross beneath its wings, swoops still closer above the treetops, apparently with the attitude that its present prey did not satisfy its palpability or not half enough to satisfy the old hungry instinct.

A small brick building, used for storing wines and groceries for the French soldiers and which up until midnight last night looked too strong and steady as to challenge anything that the enemy might have to deliver, no longer boasts its erectness but instead is in the form of a demolished building, its composition lying scattered over the surface for several yards distant all round.

Continuing towards the dugout, I notice a horse lying at the foot of a tree, his head swung at least two feet above the ground by a rope fastened to the tree. Its mate stands only a few feet away tied to another tree. The brute keeps its head in constant upward and downward motion and exposes its teeth as if in response to an unpleasant odor. The animal no doubt gestured in response to extreme pain for as I pass further to its rear, I am attracted by its entrails that have spilled out and hang almost to the ground through a large opening in its flank caused by a fragment of a shell.

Now that I have come in view of two of the dugouts, I find that the covering of one of them has been blown almost away. No doubt the men in it lie dead as a result of having been jarred to death by the concussion of the shell that fell upon it. Shells, a little less numerous than a few hours previous, still pour down upon the ground with vociferous reports. Trees and undergrowth that yesterday stood gleaming with life while flittering their green leaves with the moving breezes now seem to sob from having to give up their part or all their green life to unrelenting steel that came tearing through, unexpectedly, at midnight sharp to gore and ruin everything that dared block its path in its mad effort to clear the way for an easy march at the pleasure of the grey uniforms into Paris. The very report of the unmerciful barrage that falls near and far away seems boastful enough to indicate that the enemy expects little or no resistance in its effort to increase its salient in the direction of Paris.

A Frenchman, frightened at the approach of the German infantry in a wheat field you are soon to learn about, comes running through the undergrowth, pointing in the direction of the advancing enemy and repeating the word "boche." It must mean that he expects the whole thing to get on the retreat or sacrifice their lives at the hands of determined Germans.

I am, by this time, close to the safer dugout and call upon all the energy I have left to carry me to the interior. A few feet from the dugout, I hear a machine-gun open up a little to its rear; leaves and twigs give way to the bullets that cut and whistle through the limbs; and it is now that I can really understand that the Germans are upon us; upon us with the determination that we will die or become their prisoners in lessening their resistance to reach Paris—their hungry goal.

Coming inside the dugout, my attention is especially drawn by all the men lying flat on their bellies. I first conclude that their actions are due to fright; but I finally learn that it is through response to the shells that had previously fallen upon the dugout that they take such action, as such action eliminates the concussion of shell dropping upon the dugout. Full of pain and from being sick also, I fall upon the ground complaining loudly in response to ailments. Should the same complaints have visited me back home, I am very certain the doctor would have announced his uncertainty of my recovery. I hear someone say "He is hit or scared to death." I reply by saying "It's both." I do not mean to make a "cute" reply, either. It is actually that I am scared beyond my wits and, of course, as you have learned, been severely jarred by a shell.

I am not alone so far as physical complaint is concerned. A small guy severely shocked by one of the shells that fell upon the dugout bleeds at the nose and complains of hurting all over. I suppose this particular incident must have been what really sent them all to lying on their bellies.

My strength being completely gone and pain so intense, I do not feel that I can do more than become a useless prisoner for the Germans. Possibly an hour's relaxation and rest might bring some strength back to my body and ease my pain. But it is not hoped that I will have even a few minutes in which to relax, because I learn that the Germans are almost upon us and even a machine-gun has our range and is pestering us with a fusillade of bullets. And then I wonder why it is that we in this dugout remain and don't resist the attack. It must all be for a purpose but for what purpose I do not know and maybe it is best I do not. I again hear that machine-gun cackling—cackling with less audibility than when

I was outside. And it seems that I hear even more than one announcing an abrupt approach as the excitement grows more intense. Perhaps it all amounts to nothing more than a series of illusions; and still, too, it can as easily be real for it is a known fact that the enemy is moving upon us. Right at this crucial moment a lieutenant—yes, lieutenant Singletary it is, bounces up to the entrance of the dugout, slings someone's pack inside and yells "Get out of there quick for they are coming." Just anyone would know the significance of these words. Again and again he storms at us until all are out of the dugout save the guy that bleeds at the nose. All men, save possibly the lieutenant, are excited as they expect every moment a shell to swoop down upon them. The lieutenant could easily be misjudged as being excited; but he really is not. He only acts that way in order to concentrate the men's minds on what he is telling them and to get them to act in hurried response. His very first order after assembling us is to be sure that our rifles are loaded. The bang of the bombs and chatter of the machine-guns throws the lieutenant's platoon into such extreme mental disturbance that it is hard for them to grasp and execute his commands. A bomb landing nearby causes disorder among the men and several again seek safety back in the dugout. At this point, the lieutenant's commands become intensely harsh and again the men quickly emerge from the dugout. It is the captain who has ordered the lieutenants to take firing positions in the trenches. And it is he who intends to check the German advance even if it costs a heavy sacrifice of men and supplies.

9

Occupying France

We move in single file in the direction of the trenches as Lieutenant Singletary heads the platoon. The few moments' relaxation I get in the dugout must have somewhat recuperated me, as I am again on the move. But before proceeding very far, I happen onto some more misfortune in that I lose my footing on the wet ground, bumping my knee against a large stone that protrudes about six inches out of the ground. In the fall, the muzzle of my rifle connects with the ground, leaving a few inches of dirt in the barrel. It is a miracle that controls my faculties enough to remember to remove the dirt; but I do remember to and remove it by the use of a switch while traveling to the trench. The trench being located just beyond the swamp, we quickly take up same and await the appearance of the enemy before opening fire.

Fog hangs heavily in the wheat field below, through which the Germans are supposed to be advancing. A large fire to the left and in the direction of a town called Crezancy reveals that a house is being razed. It was no doubt set on fire by a bomb. Falling bombs become less frequent right in the vicinity of the trench. But in the vicinity of the town, that yet is not very visible through fog, bombs are falling in great numbers. To our right, machine-guns are reporting with a daring fire. To the right is a swamp of trees and underbrush and it is probably through this concealment that the German machine-gunners dare venture so close. Machine-gun bullets whistle over the trench more often every minute; and frequently, also, bullets from in front of the trench zip over our heads. These are surely rifle bullets, for the bangs of a small firearm are easily heard down there in the wheat. I figure it is folly to expose the body or any part of it above the parapet until there is something in sight to shoot at. Not only this, but I have resolved before ever seeing the firing line to observe every precaution. I know not to become too inactive. A man to my immediate right seems to care little about careless chances, and as a result keeps peeking above the parapet almost continuously. I go as far as to tell him of the danger in the action he pursues; but he remains persistent and within less than a half hour he crouches down in the trench with a bullet in his forehead, a German victim.

The men in my immediate vicinity are again much at unease as a result of a shell falling just to the rear of the trench, sprinkling them with dirt and rock fragments. Again the same thing happens and the men are beginning to feel they are in as much danger now as ever.

German planes hum low in battle formation, dropping bombs in the swamp to the rear. Everyone is commanded to lie low in the trench in order that the planes might fail to see us. Bullets whistle over the parapet more numerously than ever and it is evident that something more serious is to take place within a short while. The bombs having been dropped, the German planes circle in the direction of Crezancy, where they are lost to view.

The fog having disappeared, someone sights the advancing Germans pressing their way through the wheat in our direction. But it is not until the Germans come still closer that we open fire, at which time they distribute themselves at wide intervals in the wheat. They in return open fire with mad resistance and the fight starts in earnest. Firing my second shot, I learn that my rifle barrel has burst. Hence, I procure the dead man's rifle and open fire with the rest of the doughboys. But it is when bullets come too close to my head that I duck into the trench for safety lest my head or helmet receive a present from the enemy down yonder hidden in the wheat. It is not certain just how large a number of Germans there are in the field; but judging from the number of bullets that whistle over, there must be a pretty fair army of them. Why shoot when you see nothing to shoot at? This must be what the officers think about and as a result we are ordered to cease firing until the Germans try to advance or until they are seen. They are hidden in the wheat and it is not until they move and shake the straw that we can tell just where they are. The Germans themselves cease firing and unless something unforeseen happens, it seems that both sides will hold what he has until darkness renders it possible for either side to stretch and get a long breath. Frequent falling of shells help to keep green my memory of the last several hours. It is very certain that shells would be falling here now with, probably, only a few less in number, were it not for the German infantry itself that is so close to us. No one but a thoughtless fellow would attempt to expose his person above the parapet. But there is undoubtedly a thoughtless fellow a few yards to my left. For, in spite of discouragement to the contrary, he remains obstinate and insists he is going back to a spring for water. I think he is firm in his belief that the Germans do not intend shooting any more. So it is that he perches himself upon the surface in the rear of the trench and then falls back into the trench with a bullet through his thigh. His having no control at all of his left leg reveals that the bone is broken. A few men nearby strip his trousers down and apply first aid treatment against a heavy flow of blood. The man has plenty of courage all right, for as the men assist him in dressing the wound and stopping the flow of blood, he brings down curses on the Germans while he smokes and puffs in independent fashion. He might have realized the seriousness of his condition at first; but in the event he didn't, he surely must realize it now due to a big loss of blood that has sapped his vitality, and that has rendered his condition precarious. He no longer curses the enemy out there but lies slumped back on his pack, eyes almost set in their sockets and face so pale that he could easily be mistaken for dead. No man can live out of this trench and so why try and move him to an infirmary when it would only result in loss of lives? Hence, it results in his having to remain in the trench until darkness makes it possible to remove him.

By twelve o'clock, the fog and rain disappear and the sun beams down upon the stony trench with such heat that most of us remove our blouses in order to more comfortably endure it. The dead man to my right is removed from the trench by being whirled out upon the surface to the rear. By the middle of the afternoon, the blood from the wounded man begins to decay, creating a stinking odor that causes several nearby to adjust gas masks. It is indeed a nasty mess that goes along with winning wars; but it might have been a lot nastier had the enemy thought he would have had any chance by attacking us. To have climbed the steep slope, the Germans would have only been pretty targets for us. They act wisely by lying breathlessly in the wheat until something showed up to shoot at. While Crezancy is fully a half mile away, it is in plain view of the trench and nearly all the houses can be seen from our lofty perch. Suddenly the German artillery adjusts its range upon the town and madly bombards it for at least an hour. The town is swamped with smoke and dust and the houses in the outer portions of it, only, can be seen. Often, these houses are struck by shells crumbling down sending a screen of dust high into the air. Shells screaming from across the Marne pass over our heads and on either side of us a second later lighting in Crezancy, doing their share of damage to the town with bombastic reports and in response to the Germans' wishes. It is indeed an exciting but horrible picture. One who is able to visualize the expense of building such a town can readily sympathize with the losers. For a month or more, the people of this town have not lived there because they knew this German attack was coming. Surely, this town's people took refuge in other sections because they figured the invincible Germans would sweep through to Paris like a wave, swamping everything in their path.

It is while the town is being bombarded that someone notices a body of Germans strutting down through the wheat field as though there is nothing in front of them to give them any trouble. They walk with such grey stride as to cause one to wonder if they mean any offense by it. But offense or no offense, we open fire on them only to receive a swarm of bullets in return after they have fallen down in the wheat. More than any time previous, I realize that the German infantrymen mean to fight. Bullets zip above and beat against the parapet with stubborn resistance as each enemy returns the fire. The best we can do is shoot where we last saw the Germans. For it is impossible to see them for the wheat. Every so often wheat can be seen shaking as a result of a crawling German. Thereupon he receives a shower of bullets. In one instance, a single German takes to running in the direction of a small patch of woods in the rear of the wheat field. He is soon brought down, at which time a dozen or more men claim the honor, should it be called such.

It is quite fascinating to notice how quickly every man submerges after shooting two or three times. They know that there is danger out there and that is not any great reason why they should risk their bodies above the parapet very long at the time unless the enemy is advancing. It is indeed a wise old head that said "Here on this abrupt incline this trench shall be dug." For right here the enemy cannot help but die should he undertake to advance.

As I slowly emerge my head above the parapet, I happen to notice three Germans run behind an old ammunition cart that seems to have been hit by a shell and rendered useless. I shoot five times at the spot where I see them fall. This, apparently a slow process through the use of an ordinary rifle, I procure the rifle the wounded man is forced to abandon which to my delight is a Chau-Chau rifle that operates kind of on the same principle of a machine-gun and repeats eighteen times. Quickly focusing my rifle upon the ammunition cart, I sprinkle it and its immediate surroundings with eighteen bullets. I quickly reload and repeat with eighteen more. I carry on this repetition for about five minutes, at which time I think I have done all the damage I can there and then retire below the parapet for awhile.

The barrage having stopped, Crezancy is again visible from my point of observation. The smoke and dust seem to have disappeared within a few minutes' time. It is easy to discern that the town is demolished, every house seeming to have been blown down or at least rendered entirely useless. I am reminded of pictures of the old ruins of Rome. My mind will forever remain green with the memories of seeing Crezancy laid to waste and its picture after being destroyed.

It seems a miracle that the invincible Germans should have stopped, even, at the resistance of the steep hill or you might say small mountain and our assistance this morning. I am sure the Germans must be as tired from having to lie so quietly in the wheat as we are from having to remain so confined in the trench.

10

Night of the 15th

Darkness gradually comes on, spreading a blanket between us and the enemy. It is then that we dare stretch our muscles and yawn as gestures for relief. But even now a bullet or shell might sweep through to put a climax to the catastrophe. The wounded man is carried from the trench barely alive and it is expected that he will soon take quarters in the land beyond the clouds.

The day's confinement in the trench finds my canteen empty and me very thirsty as a result. Hence, I am inspired to go back a little way to where I know there is a spring and get some water. Darkness shields me; therefore, I do not feel that I will be a target for the Germans in the field below. It is when I begin walking that I can so easily tell how weak I am from my morning's experiences. I am sore from head to foot and in addition feel feverish and dizzy as I trudge along under the most disgusting moments I ever thought of ever experiencing. Coming near the spring, an object can be seen lying by the water. Closer observation reveals an American soldier who has been killed and lies on belly with face submerged in the water. I act to the contrary in getting the water, thereby returning to the trench only to wish later that I had drunk all I could and filled my canteen with it.

After complete darkness, we are ordered out of the trench to take temporary positions about a hundred yards further back. It is reported that the captain expects a machine-gun and rifle barrage by the Germans later in the night and intends to trick them by pulling his men back of the positions the Germans know about. He, the captain, acts wisely when he pulls his Company a little south of the forest on the slope of the incline. For the Germans do come across with a machine-gun and rifle barrage during the night. And never before had I imagined so many bullets could be manufactured. They zip through the trees by the thousands as our hearts beat harmony with their tune. To my left, right in a strip of woods across an opening, I can see the flash of a machine-gun as it spits out bullets to excite its enemy to the belief that the Germans mean to walk on to Paris and that there is no need of resisting their efforts. Then, through effort to mock his cocky pride, I turn my rifle upon his fiery position and at the finish of my round, scuttle down the incline until I am sure that I am safe in the event he turns the barrage upon me.

Down at the foot of the incline, our cannons bark and bang, whirling bombs to the enemy on the other side of the Marne. It is some comfort at least to know that they are receiving what we have for so long received and what we above all most dread. Bursting shells to the rear roar their disapproval of our not retreating and were it not that the Germans are so close to us they would no doubt give us a thrill similar to that of last night. The shells seem to play jokes on their senders when they fall in meatless territory belching blazing streaks on bursting.

The late hours of night find the German fire practically ceased save, maybe, a half-dozen machine-guns that keep vigil over the doughboys who have restrained from shooting extensively. Now and then a shell drops in the woods or nearby to remind the khakis that all have not yet inhabited the land of dreams the other side of the Marne. Yes, and now and then back in the beriddled forest of the ever-to-be famous Marne a machine-gun can be heard barking as though to pull down the curtain and sprawl back into slumber darkness. Then its bullet snipes pass over our heads as much as to say "Maybe we can add a bug to our craws through accident." Back down in homeless Crezancy, shells at several minute intervals bang sharply upon the vast waste doing no possible harm other than causing the night to seem hellish and absent of civilization anywhere in France.

The only pleasant thoughts for several days to buzz into our ears, and from an unknown source, are those to the effect that the Germans are thought to be retreating back across the Marne and possibly further back than general opinion would admit. The opinion is that for the purpose of retreating the German artillery laid Crezancy to waste. And added opinion is that the German machine-guns that entertain us out there in the forest incessantly bark to shield the fact that our enemy is on the retreat.

As the machine-guns cluck taps and as the scattering night hawks swoop down banging sentimental harmony with former, I lean back upon my pack dropping off into restful slumber, to be awakened in the early morning with rain drops beating reveille against my facial anatomy. My mind clicks with disgust to find myself stretched under the relentless mercy of the determined enemy after relishing a dream that I was back in civilization no longer a victim for torment. Even now machine-guns can be heard barking back in the distant forest, as shells report with sharp explosions, occasionally at close quarters but more numerously in the distance. Air-machines span the air with guttural effort to determine some definite purpose: maybe to learn the results of yesterday's actions.

11

Awaiting Orders

But we cannot afford to lie sprawled in the open to be observed and located by the curious German birdmen lest we become subject to the merciless bomb hawks that swoop down and carry off its prey before the victim has time to even adjust his muscles preparatory to evading being clawed in two. Hence, we are instructed to take up the trenches still further back but to the right of our present positions. The instructions are carried out immediately and the trench is occupied within less time than ten minutes. To our immediate right are French infantrymen who apparently take conditions with less remorse than any American in France. Those who smoke do so with the ease and comfort of any lounging countrymen in America. And it is only at the report of a shell nearby that one diddles his foot through unconscious response.

A red squirrel playing in front of the trench is quite fascinating to watch as its movements seem to indicate that it has forgotten that yesterday its natural home stood a subject to its most determined and most deadly enemy.

Early-morning patrolmen report the absence of any Germans this side of the Marne. A dreadful pain that for so many hours has overhung the minds of the American infantrymen now for the most part vanishes. Even a smile, a broad smile shapes itself upon the faces of all the boys. No sir, no one but he who never saw inside of a trench or heard a shell flash its resentful bitterness, would dare drag a scowl across his face and say "Ah Hell. I knew that's the way it would turn out!" On the contrary, we hope that's the way it turns out all the way back to Berlin. But still, it is hard to clear the mind of the doubt that the Germans are beaten. Indeed, the invincible must have something trickery up their sleeves that they mean to deal out just when we are in the height of entertaining a misconception.

The American and French artillery plays the important role throwing bombs swishing and squealing through the air to light and tear up something with bombastic thunderation the other side of the silent Marne. Occasionally, the enemy spats back with a little scattering resistance falling generally to the rear of the reserve trenches.

As for orders, I doubt that the lieutenants know any more about the intentions of the higher officers than we buck privates. The question is asked by everyone, "What will happen next?" It is possible that the battalion commander only knows the next move the battalion will take. The lieutenants, or shave tails, as they are often spoken of, seem in as much suspense as the rest of the soldiers. Here we are huddled and concentrated in this trench hovering over suspense only knowing that there is something to be done. What? We will find out surely, not maybe. The odor from withering leaves and high explosives is nauseating. Severe headaches develop among the men as they remain crouched in the trench while they await orders that will put the battalion into action or relief. One witty but disgusted doughboy breaks the monotony by announcing that he will try another cigarette, for that is all to be gotten in this man's land. Another replies by adding "Yes when you can get 'em; and listen, suppose you save me a drag on that one." His remark is enough to indicate that he is out of cigarettes. Let me tell you, this is no place to be out of smoking tobacco in the event one is a smoker. Too bad, too bad! For any time a shell screams close by or shakes the ground with its concussion, that smoker is sure to be excited into this desirous conscience at which time he can nervously gulp down a barrel of smoke. Oh, yes! Because that good old smoke does so much to steady the nerves; or to say the least, play a role of satisfaction somehow.

Afternoon finds us still snugged away in the trench, but we have received the news that we are to comb the forest all the way to the river in order to determine definitely if the Germans have really retired to the other side. Everything ready for the move and with bayonet flipping their glare with shiny streaks, we pull slowly out of the trench and trudge in a wave towards the famous river.

There is really felt a kick in my veins as my blood flows with curiosity as to just what is going to be the outcome of our occupational adventure through doubtful forest that has hidden in it—who knows—? Let's hope that they are all dead, or if we are to give them the breaks, that they have made it possible for the river to separate us. Men move in hordes in quiet advance. A general glance upon their faces reveals the uncertainty that they carry along with the advance; uncertainty as to the enemy's previous actions; uncertainty as to the future. Even I have bred more serious thoughts within the last several hours than all the rest of my life put together. The thoughts of ever having been cruel and abusive to poor helpless dumb animals bring with them repentance and conscious promises that such will never be repeated if only I can be spared from the hells that are all the time holding death in one hand and our fates in the other.

Yes, it is this mess of spouting geysers and banging shells that awakens me with consciousness of his puny and worthless past. If by miracle, tomorrow the War-Gods should call it finis, who would profit by his sad and cruel experiences of last night and today? Whose past way of living and walk of life would be abruptly displaced by something entirely different; by something that would be a blessing to himself and all those participating in the same social and environmental changes.

With these and many more similar thoughts flashing through my mind, I suddenly come across a slain French soldier lying by the side of a small path. His face half torn off by a shell fragment, the remainder of his head and his shoulders lie saturated in the blood spilled upon the ground; the mortal wound leaving his be-ragged teeth, brains and bones exposed to view, and his blue uniform a nasty mess. The observer involuntarily realizes the ferocity with which the enemy bites. Blowflies apparently fight for supremacy over the remains of the slain hero and soon his whole body can be nothing more than a mass of maggots, each striving for his share of the German victim. The fact that the Frenchman's shoes have been taken, seems to me to be indicative that the enemy is none too flush with leather with which to supply the demand.

One sergeant looking upon the dead figure shapes his lips into a sarcastic smile and says "So that's the way it turned out for you, Eh?" Should the slain victim return to life again hearing this curt remark, he might retaliate with words very unpleasant to the sergeant and remind him that he too might drink and wallow in his own blood before nightfall spreads a blanket of darkness over his countenance. Who knows at what moment a machine-gun might announce its bitterness to our approach with a thousand bullets peppering upon us without one word of warning. The machine-gunners might now be smiling while they watch us trudge into one of their own prepared traps. They will then laugh even more after having lain us upon the ground, forever to remain. It is some relief on hearing our batteries drop bombs upon the relentless enemy somewhere over there. But where, just where I certainly do not know. And the brave attitude the captain displays is almost as encouraging as the sound of the battering themselves, his indomitable spirit and courage and inspiration enough to cause the men to somewhat take on the ire that it will be just a walkover. One of the sergeants, but not the one spoken of above, has previously been awfully daring; I mean daring up until last night when the Germans defied his unlikable personality. But now he seems more meek and complains of being shell shocked. It is whispered among the men that he is just a plain case of cowardice and using his complaint as an alibi. I do not mean to compare all the Company sergeants with the two I have spoken of and left unnamed. Most of them are daring and courageous under fire and honest in their efforts to beat the enemy all the way back to Germany.

But turning from this side of the question, a dead German draws my attention as he lies on his belly as if taking a nap; hence, his appearance does not have the mental effect as that of the Frenchman. The German's helmet lies a few feet distance from the body and half bent, evidently from being hit by a shall fragment.

12

The Barrier

Further penetration of the forest reveals that the trees and under-growth have undergone a terrible siege of machine-gun and shell fire. Large trees lie wholly upon the ground or half-felled upon other trees or undergrowth by shells that came rambling through last night. It is hard to find a spot on a tree large enough to place a hand that has not been scarred by shrapnel. Frequently, limbs can be heard or seen falling when a slow wind passes through the forest. This is due to limbs so nearly having been broken off that the least disturbance completes the effect. The ground is pulverized in most places and in several instances, pieces of wood and roots torn from the ground are to be seen lodged high in the limbs of trees. The barrage was tremendous and it is unreasonable to imagine anything could have lived through this merciless barrage laid down by the Germans to destroy everything from men on down in their selfish effort to gulp Paris and in fact all France that their power might everlastingly become definitely invincible, indomitable. Further occupation of the swamp brings to light more of last night's destructiveness. Trees and in fact any form of inanimate life seems to be stirring under mad disgust of the debaucheries of it all. Hideous has the once beautiful scenery become; become such overnight. It is enough to debauch and seduce those willpowers that carry the least characteristic of weakness; but it could be worse, for how easily could we be trudging under blasting artillery fire. If such could be the case or might become the case, what could be worse, there being no holes to crawl in nor no possibility of running from approaching shells.

The battalion comes to an almost abrupt halt when it becomes impossible to advance through a wide cluster of saplings bent over almost to the ground and tied and tangled together so scientifically as to baffle even a small boy. It would be nothing more than sheer prejudice-ness not to admit this action wise on the part of the enemy. We can do nothing more than seek a sector of easier resistance; or should I say a sector of possible advance? There is no exaggeration when I say that a small hog would have a tough time making his way through the leafy and branchy entanglement. At this point of interruption, we are ordered to fall out for awhile. While various conversations are being held among the men, most of which are very uninteresting, I silently draw my own conclusions as to the meaning of this act (entanglement handicap) the Germans have pulled on us. My conclusions are that the enemy's intentions are to check us until it has time to complete a successful retreat or fortify itself against our attack. The conclusions are very simple, I think.

The men still enjoy their smoking and begin complaining that their tobacco is running low. As they lie here awaiting further action, at least five or six drag off the same cigarette until the last one to drag burns his lips in an effort to draw enough smoke to enjoy four or five good inhalations.

One guy through response to a shell that creates discontent among us by bursting close by says "Hell, I guess it's started all over again." Almost at the same moment he completes his statement, another lights close by with vociferous report and at this juncture, the same fellow says "Now by-god I know it has." Well, this is funny to say the least and could be enjoyed immensely were it not that the fear of another or more just like the other two might bang down so close that things might become miserable. Now a fellow, a Jew by birth, brings about most comedy through his telling of last night's experiences. The Jew reiterates that he never before prayed; but that he prayed last night and prayed fast and hard. He puts emphasis on his contentions when he repeatedly says "You could have heard my voice above the bursting shells." While the Jew, no doubt, intends to exaggerate a little on this particular statement, he, as a rule, is very sincere in what he says; especially about having never prayed until the shells begin to pop last night at which time most all of us asked the aid of the spiritual supreme. His telling of the captain having fired him from being mess sergeant, climaxes our guffaws as we adjust ourselves in readiness to move in response to the captain's command.

12. The Barrier

Our forward movement being blocked, we move parallel with the entanglement until it is reported we will intersect a road leading toward the river. The blockade continues general and the barrier has rendered it indeterminate as to whether or not the main German body has retreated all the way across the river. However, it is still generally believed that the enemy no longer occupies the swamp on our side of the river but has retreated across to use the river as a barrier to stop our advance that it surely must know we meant to make.

The middle of the afternoon brings us to the road that I have learned connects the Marne River and Crezancy. The road is laden with trees either felled by shells or by axes. It is impassable for traffic; men afoot only, can pass over it. Tonight, it is reported the engineers will clear the road of the barriers. The 3rd. Division has for the most part moved up closer to the river in pursuit of the retreating enemy. Our right flank has been hinging on Blesmy Farm but now flanks the forest to the right as far down as the barrier of saplings. We are also occupying the heights overlooking the Marne and at this point the hill on which we checked the Germans the morning of the 15th is visible. Smoke from the ashes of the few buildings razed by fire caused from explosives in and in the near vicinity of Crezancy can also be seen as it creeps above the treetops that hides Crezancy from our view. No longer do shells bang upon devastated Crezancy, although it is not at all impossible. The German shellfire centers nearer the river and in territory to the right of the road leading to the river. Sharp reports of bombs can be heard further up the river swamp. I feel that the Germans are settling down on the other side of the Marne to give us an unwelcome reception if ever upon that other side we dare occupy. But we will not even attempt to occupy it today, the 16th of July. We are too completely cut off to even entertain such an idea. Tomorrow maybe; the next day maybe; I can't say just when but it will happen. You will learn about it later. Now lounging upon the ground awaiting further instructions, some of us become rather restless; restless from wallowing around upon uncomfortable ground and not restless from wanting to fight Germans. Therefore, we wander out into the bushes, not through curiosity, but through desire to move about. I do not wander far from the lounging Company for fear that we will be called into order any minute. Looking upon the large acreage of fine trees, some of which have their trunks and limbs gnawed beyond valuation, I, even though my mind is shocked and its faculties rendered so disorderedly as to destroy clear thinking, do manage to concentrate, for a moment, upon the miserable thought that civilization must be no more, lest this barbarous destructive act should not have been. This vast amount of devastated waste is only a mite compared with all the forest, farms and towns and cities that have been ruined since the war started. Here, in the very tops of trees, are limbs made conspicuous from being scarred in large wounds by the tremendous shellfire of night before last. The odor from explosives, gas and withering leaves is more nauseating than ever; and thanks that it does not contract a headache for me as it has for so many of the other men.

Now, in the midst of my narrow adventure, I am attracted by a four-cornered masonry of stone that as most anyone would, on first sight, take to be an old well guard. The first of a series of questions that pass through my mind is what would be the object of a well in such an isolated forest? It being impossible to draw upon any purpose of the well being here, should it prove out to be a well, I dismiss all questions from my mind and resolve, through investigation, to satisfy my own curiosity. Again, my mind is attracted, this time by a fixed bayonet that is very splotched with dry blood and lies about ten feet distant from the masonry. This is my first evidence of a hand-to-hand engagement, this undoubtedly having been one the morning of the 15th but apparently longer ago than that. The blood stains show that the bayonet pierced its antagonist a little better than half its length. It might be interesting, but disappointing as it were, to tell you that I later learned the victorious rifle was that used by the enemy. Calling one of my comrades, who has wandered off a little way in another direction, to the scene, he picks up the rifle and sniffing the stink of the rotten blood, throws it down quickly saying "Ain't this a hell of a way for people to kill each other?" "It is," says I, "and I hope I never have to engage in this bayonet fighting they talk about."

"So do I" says he. Neither is he reluctant in laying emphasis on the fact that he does not care about any of it. For he in as many words says, "We had no business coming over here anyway. This weren't none of the United State's business to butt in."

12. The Barrier

He full looks his contempt and displays his disgust of it all. Just at this point of our conversation, a shell is heard squealing with mad velocity landing close enough by to shake the leaves nearby and to rekindle, to some extent, the same fear we so nervously nursed night before last. Both of us on hearing the shell approaching, quickly take quarters in a nearby shell hole where my companion more nervously falls curses upon that "Damned old Kaiser" while I listen on with no kind regard of old Kaiser myself.

My companion, apparently satisfied that Kaiser and this and that one who is responsible for this war, feel the curses of an unknown source conveyed by the spiritual curses, turns his face quickly in the direction of the rifle saying, "I have been told these Heinies never leave their dead behind because they don't want 'em to know how many of 'em got killed." "But" says he, "I don't know if they get 'em every one. Do you reckon they do?"

"Well no." says I. "I know they don't succeed in recovering every dead boy; as a matter of fact I have already seen one dead German myself. However, I wouldn't be a bit surprised if they conceal as many of the dead as possible in order to destroy evidence of their actual loss." "Well!" he says gruffly but still with a countenance on which is written an unusual personality and good character. "I can't understand why they are able to hold out so well. Looks like they ought to know they can't whip the whole world."

"But you know they have been preparing so long a time with all this in view," I say.

"Yes, system and preparation goes a long way; but you know so many men can get killed off till nothing won't do no good."

"Yes" says I, "but maybe their system enables them to kill off ten of their enemy while their enemy is killing off only one or two of them."

"Right you may be," he exclaims, "but before it is all over we will be killing ten of them to their one."

"Killing ten to one" I exclaim, "Thought you said we had no business in this man's war."

"Why hell," he exclaims, "we can kill 'em just the same if we don't have any business in it can't we?"

47

I like this humor and reply by saying "I guess we can do that all right."

It is through this statement that I can easily discern that my good comrade is in sympathy heart and soul with the U.S.A. and all those allies with it.

Still anxious to satisfy my curiosity about the masonry of stone, I cannot refrain from casting my eye in that direction very often while we are conversing. Now his curiosity becoming aroused, he says, "Why do you keep looking out that way so often for?"

"Looking out that way nothing," I reply, "I am looking at that small structure of stone there. What do you think I am looking at?"

"Oh," says he, "I thought you were looking at something beyond that."

"No, hardly anything beyond that," I say. "That must be an old well and it is funny it hasn't been knocked down before now by a shell," I continue.

"Yes but funny things will happen. And do you know," he says, "that out there on that road there is a mounted statue of Christ that wasn't even touched during this barrage and everything around about it was torn all to pieces?"

"I didn't notice that," I reply.

"Yes," says he, "It's right there not touched. Not even scratched. And do you know that certainly does look funny to me that such a thing should happen?"

Gesturing to the stones, I say, "But you see that well curbing is larger than any mounted statue of Christ, I should think, and it is not torn up." "But" I add, "it is a wonder isn't it?

"A wonder it is," he replies, "but you see it is scarred up very much."

"It is at that," I reply.

He suddenly changes the subject by frankly admitting that he had far rather be a street cleaner back in Missouri than a sergeant in any man's army.

"A sergeant you say you are? Where are your stripes?" I ask. For I have by this time noticed that he didn't have any.

"My stripes, Why! I don't wear any stripes. These damned Germans pick at all the officers. Didn't you know that?"

12. The Barrier

"At officers? You mean they pick at commissioned officers. Those that wear leather leggings and gold and silver insignias."

"The devil" he says, "They pick at any leaders and not only that, they kill 'em too if they get a chance." He chuckles.

At first I believe the sergeant to be trying to kid me into thinking he is important, but I am wrong. The sergeant really is in earnest about what he has to say concerning the Germans killing all leaders. It is not through vain-ness that he takes this attitude. He is a real man.

"You say you are from Missouri? I take that you must be since you said you had rather be a street cleaner in one of the Missouri towns than a sergeant in this army."

"I am," says he.

"Well we are kinda neighbors at that," I say, "as I am a Louisianan myself."

The fact that the sergeant is more willing to hold a good old conversation than most sergeants, causes me to create a liking for him. He talks freely about his sister and mother who he says depend upon him for support. It is easy to discern that his affection for them is unlimited.

"I hope I don't get killed here in France as I want to go back and educate my sister. She is a bright kid and anxious about getting an education," he says.

But it is not meant that the sergeant should return to carry out his much desired intentions. The tragic end he finally met closes the curtain to all his hopes and ambitions.

The sergeant, whose name I learn is Easterday, is still full of talk when the whistle sounds to fall-in. The interruption brings us both to our feet, at which time I rush to the structure of stone to see what it all really means. Looking quickly over into the inside, the stinking odor of two dead Frenchmen gushes into my face such as to almost make my legs sag. I suppose this is the result of a bayonet engagement. And yet I do not know the purpose of the masonry of stone.

Returning to the Company, Captain Woodside informs us that the barrier of saplings has rendered it impossible to reach the river and that we will retire to Crezancy until such time as it takes to receive further instructions.

13

Crezancy

The captain's announcement fills everyone with joy, removing the frowns of disgust with smiles that float about on their pleasing countenances. One fellow remarks that maybe they have a canteen in the town and it might be possible to buy some cigarettes. "Guess he must have some money" I think. "Cigarettes! What could I do towards satisfying myself with cigarettes even if I smoked and not a franc in my pocket or no indication of any money soon." These are my thoughts and thanks that we are not pestered with inviting canteens or other nice things for sale since I and most all the rest have no money.

Never before had I seen a town completely demolished. Only have I witnessed such scenes through pictures. But now I would get to see demolished Crezancy. A horrible picture, surely, but still since it all had to be, it can be nothing short of a thrill to look upon the ruins.

A little hiking alongside the road carries us from among so many trees and underbrush and into the road where felled trees no longer block it to traffic. But trees are not all that have been felled in the road. Men, horses, a few mules and lorries block the road in places. Wagons lie bottom side up either shaped so by bombs or turned over by the animals pulling it in their haste caused by the bombs that poured down upon the road the night of the barrage. All horses killed lie either hitched to wagons or else with rigging on them to indicate that they had been pulling drayage but tore loose on being excited by shells, to be killed later. A most cruel and hideous picture is witnessed in one instance, a horse's belly having been ripped by a shell fragment, the animal through pain and excitement shows that it fled dragging its entrails, tearing them out with its feet until it fell dead.

The road is torn up and rendered useless by the unmerciful bombs that tore everything into shreds the night of the 14th. Men lying torn and mangled in and beside the road leads one to the belief that human beings no longer have any mercy upon one another. But this is war, and who knows that on the other side of the Marne Germans, too, might be lying ground into the soil to add to the grief of their families back in Germany. It is for democracy they say we are fighting. It's a pity but there could be a more humane way of settling the cause for right whatever it may be.

Blowflies behave like an angry hive of bees as they swarm madly over the dead animals and body of a slain man. It brings over one the solemnity experienced back in the period of adolescence when every boy seems to think that everything is always going wrong and that if the world keeps on growing worse it can't stand much longer lest a change by miracle takes place. It also brings one's memory back to his historical knowledge of how the people used to do each other in, in response to the desire for sport.

Probably four years ago the inhabitants of Crezancy never dreamed that the road connecting it and the Marne River would at this time hold the bodies of slain men that fought for its safety, and animals that also would die trudging under the whip of sometimes cruel men and hellish bombs. But most probably they began to realize that a terrible tragedy of some sort was to take place when they received word that their bitter enemy was madly closing in on their town to sack it at the cost of their lives or what not, just as it (their enemy) triumphed in its effort to force France under the lash of the Kaiser adding to Germany's domain and prestige. It was on receiving such word that Crezancy's inhabitants took refuge in some quarters more distant removed from the advancing, unconquerable enemy. Indeed, a month ago the Germans greatly increased their salient in the direction of Paris shaping it (their salient) in the form of a wedge. The French and English soldiers and French civilians not only in Crezancy but in hundreds of other towns and villages fled before the determined enemy, leaving everything behind to be destroyed or exposed of as the Heinies wished.

A few personal and necessary belongings were all that the fleeing civilians could gather in their haste to save themselves from being captured by the Germans. Even then, some of the inhabitants were taken by the enemy and kept by it, to be used as their captors wished.

The German advance brought them to the Marne, about two miles or three kilometers from Crezancy, where they established inactive fighting until they could get ready for the final drive on Paris. This meant the final drive, and it seems to be Providence that directs the cause telling or forcing the invincible to retreat that in order that so-called Justice might be spared. I can, now, imagine the Imperial Kaiser mopping his brow in response to disappointment of yesterday's outcome and frowning under disgust of his defeated army in this sector. On the other hand, I can picture the happiness among the people of the countries colleagued against Germany in effort to win what they believe to be right.

But returning to the road, we are by this time nearing the town. A cemetery is made conspicuous by the barrage. Broken and scattered marble lie over the surface in and nearby the cemetery. Hardly a whole headstone remains. I am daily attracted by the dead remains that have been torn out of the graves or tombs and lie exposed to the surface. In some instances leg bones and bones of arms lie on or protrude out of the loose ground; and some whole skeletons lie upon the ground. It reminds me of the proverb "And the dead shall rise out of their tombs." But anyone can reason that this proverb did not mean to apply here and in this manner. These and somewhat similar sights are what cause one to almost imagine that civilization and pleasantness of life have taken wings and flown away.

The first vivid view of the town reveals that a large building has been torn down for the most part by bombs. Part of the walls, only, remain. Withered limbs stand out among the live limbs of trees. Several trees lie across the road entering the town and it is necessary that we detour around them to continue our travel. Passing through a small cluster of trees, we are suddenly confronted with the torn and demolished town. The street we enter is filled with stone, limbs, broken clay shingles, strips of lathing, and in some cases broken furniture, dish pans, pieces of dishes, etc. Nothing could be more indicative that the townsmen left in great haste. All the buildings bordering the street look as if they have been dynamited, scattering their compositions in all directions. Inside the remaining walls, stone, dust, and debris of many sorts are piled up presenting a devastating, ragged, and nasty appearance. A very disagreeable odor has developed as a result of rain having fallen on the debris causing fermentation and rotting of the contents of stores and houses.

It is only in a very few cases that even parts of the tops of buildings remain. Every house has been hit by at least two or three bombs.

Assembling in the street as best we can to certainly not attempt lining-up, the captain gives us our orders which are for the main part to stay close around the town in the event we are called out. He orders the sergeants to find billets for their platoons to sleep in, and it is my platoon's luck to have to sleep in a cellar underneath a demolished house. But before going into telling you how we sleep, I shall tell a little more about the town.

Before the sun, which is getting low now, goes down, I resolve to do a little exploring, mainly in hunt for some fruit; for I surmise that perhaps through good fortune, there might be some left. A guy whom they call "Red" volunteers to go on the hunt with me. It is not long until we find an orchard of plums and prunes, the latter for which I have no good taste; but I help myself to the plums and a few pears. Eating to satisfaction and filling our pockets with as many plums as we care for, we agree to explore the town just to see if we can find a house unhit by a bomb. Our search reveals no un-hit houses and two live animals, a cow and a cat. The former moos lonesome as she tries to pick her way through the stone and debris. The animal looks and seems to be hungry and it is with great regret that we are unable to pacify her with something to eat. The cat rekindles our scares when it dashes out the door of a small barn we pass near. The little animal seems very frightened and proves its dissatisfaction of our presence by bouncing over a stone fence in mad haste.

"These Germans must have him scared to death too," Red says.

"Gosh!" says I, "we are not so scared, are we?"

"No!" replies Red, "not now maybe. But what about night before last?"

"Yes, I remember something about that," I say.

"Yes!" replies Red, "and you are apt to remember a lot more about it before it is all over, you just watch."

Discovering that Red is a pessimistic fellow, and in order to have a little fun, I converse as though I believe it is all over and that we will be home by Thanksgiving. But Red cannot be kidded into such improbable stuff and honestly believes the worst is yet to come; and he might be right at that.

Taking a seat on the fence the cat jumped over, and confidently sure we can hear the whistle blow in the event we were called into assemble, we continue discussing what has been and what we think might continue to be. But still I tease "Red" along the make-belief that the war is over.

"See yonder," he says. "That looks like it is all over don't it?"

It is now getting dark and it is German flare signals that Red sees going up across the river.

"What does that have to do with the war going to end or not going to end?" I say.

"That means they have something up their sleeves and there is no telling when they will surprise somebody with another blamed barrage," he says.

It is at this point that I truly quit my kidding and partly agree in my own mind that this guy might be guessing correctly: A barrage. "Who can stand another one of those things," I ask myself.

Both of us sit silently for a few minutes viewing the enemy's actions beyond the river. These signals mean something and gosh if it happens to mean another barrage. I can't live under the strain. It might mean that they know we are making our quarters here; if it is true, we are gone. Now I can almost imagine I hear them squealing through the air to fall upon us with as deadly intentions as night before last, or the night of the 14th.

The flares ascend more numerously as it grows darker and they can now be seen far to the right and left on the German front as well as directly across the river from Crezancy. We do not look at the signals altogether because we are curious as to their meaning but we are also attracted by the beautiful display they cause on ascending high into the air.

I recollect to assemble my faculties and as a result find myself imagining all kinds of bad things are going to happen right away.

13. Crezancy

"Red," I exclaim, "I refuse to grow pessimistic. I just won't believe this barrage of signals has any detrimental significance. It can as easily mean that the Germans are signaling for more profound retreat. Let us at least try and pacify our minds with the belief that everything is turning out all right until we know we face, unavoidably, the worst. If we do that we will be doing a lot better all the time."

"You can go ahead and imagine anything you want about this thing and that thing," he says, "but I know we are facing Hell here all the time and before morning, if you and I are both still alive, you will say I knowed what I was talking about."

I become convinced that Red will continue this tune all the time and as a result, I make my mind up to avoid his companionship as much as possible even though he belongs to the same squad as I; for such attitude, I conclude will lead to mental disrupt.

The Company assembly whistle interrupts our observation and in response, we hop off the fence, quickly reporting to the street. On reaching the street, we do not find the Company lining up for assembly but find the men assembled in an old barnyard across the street waiting in line for each man's ration of chow.

About the time we finish our little ration of hash and hard tack, everything becomes as lighted as though the sun itself were shining. Shadows of every object move in circular motion.

"Look at that," someone exclaims, and pointing in the direction of the German front.

Everyone turning to look, discovers that a star shell has crept up into high altitude above the enemy territory and has burst, lighting everything for miles around; and in near vicinity of the shell, the shell is so luminous that the light is as effective as the light of the sun.

This is my first vision of a star shell. Such shells are used by the enemy for quick observation purposes. And it is through means of this star shell that we in Crezancy fear we are spied upon. Every man I hear speak voices his uneasiness of this spontaneous action on the part of the Germans and like "Red" expresses his believe that everything will be blown into dust by morning. Hence, it is not hard to understand why every soldier in this devastated town passes a restless night.

But now to retire to our billets, I soon learn that together with the worry of expectation of a barrage, we are all to pass a restless night's sleep in that we are huddled all together in a small cellar to be scrounged and punched by each other all night without any fresh air to comfort our poisoned lungs, the only possibility of ventilation being the small entrance to the cellar.

Most of all the men become very contrary. Some of them curse loudly, remarking that they would rather be lying under a mad barrage than lying in such a place with not any fresh air to breathe or room to move an elbow. Red especially proclaims that it all is nothing but a peck of foolishness and frankly exclaims "I wish I was plumb back in Arkansas away from this damned place."

Someone evidently vexed at Red's perpetual complaints, says, "I had about as soon be here as in that damned country you talk about." I take it that he means by insinuating that Arkansas is no component of the United States.

Someone else interrupts by saying "Hold your peace, for if you don't the Heinies will hold it for you."

"Move that damned knee out of my ribs," another says. The antagonist replies by saying "Go to Hell."

This is about the routine of conversation that keeps vigil over the occupants of the cellar all night. And now that the night is over, it is the fresh air we so warmly welcome on our exit from the cellar. Every man seems weak and drowsy from breathing poisonous air all night. I fill my lungs several times with fresh air which I find does a great deal of good in relieving me of my dizzy and sickly feeling.

I feel very relieved to have passed the night as well as I did for so many had expressed the opinion that a barrage would visit us that I had begun to believe the contrary impossible.

Loitering around awhile, we respond to the call for chow after the finish of which we are advised by Captain Woodside that so far as he knew there would be nothing but a little drill for the Company during the day. We are glad to hear that we will get off so lightly for the captain might have probably said we would clean the street of its debris.

Our platoon sergeant salutes the captain, turns to the men and says, "I want my platoon to come with me as I have a little work for you to do."

13. Crezancy

On reaching our destination, the sergeant details his platoon to clean out a billet partly torn down by a shell. "Clean out this building," he says. "This will be our quarters while we are here." It is not long before I find that other sergeants have their platoons acting likewise.

Having removed most all the trash from our abode, we are astonished to find a nice piano buried under a lot of broken stone and trash. The building having been cleaned out, each squad selects its apartment, which in each case is in a single room for each squad. Arranging my pack in one corner of the room I select, I take position on my haunches until everyone in the squad settles on his own quarters in the room.

Now for the first time in about three days I pull my pocket mirror out and look upon my countenance which is difficult to see for my healthy growth of black whiskers. My hair is also none too primped and is full of sand and trash. I hate to admit this but, nevertheless, it is true and since I am writing it as I saw it in the trenches, I feel inclined not to omit it.

I go out to a barn and wash my head as clean as possible in a water trough and then ask the Company barber the chances of getting a haircut on a credit. The barber, apparently believing we might not get any money at all as long as we are on the lines, to say nothing if I get killed, agrees reluctantly to cut my hair. There was but little hair left on my head when he finished for I was of the opinion that it would be a long time until I got another haircut; and maybe never from this barber in the event I failed to get some money.

We are advised that since we were victorious in our engagement with the Germans we could write home about it. Most of the men are soon found writing home about the Germans retreating and how we out-fought them. One guy says, "I am going to write a whole book home about it." And I guess he did for he was writing all day to someone or more. After having procured a pencil and a little paper on which to write, I find it impossible for me to write from still being so nervous from heavy mental strain and from having been shocked the morning of the fifteenth. Hence, it is necessary for me to get someone to write for me while I dictate the news home that I had lived through it and that the enemy was on the run.

A few papers, printed in English, are brought up from Paris telling of the Marne battle. The headlines of the paper "Germans in Full Retreat Closely Pursued by the Americans" are sensationally conspicuous. This headline is very inspiring indeed but our inspirations become a little dwindled when we read further that the Germans are thought to be entrenched in the Belleau country, their intentions being to stop the American and French advance if possible. The paper goes on to describe the bravery and courage of the gallant American soldiers, their fresh entry into the war and their determination not to be stopped by the Germans but on the other hand to put the Germans on the retreat and quickly end the war.

A fellow who apparently had not yet mailed his letter home says, "I want to get that paper and mail the clipping about the fight to my people."

A sarcastic lieutenant replies, "Send the clipping home? Don't your people ever get newspapers? Every paper in America is full of this stuff about this battle and you ought to know that." He speaks the last sentence as he walks away folding the paper and putting it into his pocket.

Having read the paper or rather having heard it read by the lieutenant, the men remain huddled together discussing its contents for awhile. They are interrupted by the sound for chow, it being about midday, at which event every man grabs his mess-kit and starts for the kitchen. The kitchen is always spoken of as the rolling kitchen because it is transferred along with the Company on wheels; that is, so long as the Company is not on an active firing line.

Chow being finished, I suggest to two fellows that we walk about over the town a little and thence to the field where we engaged the Germans the morning of the 15th. They agree and in a demolished building we find a bottle of purple ink. We carve our names on our helmets by mean of nails and then paint over the initials with the ink by means of a small stick. The finish of a little more exploring of the town finds us on our way to the battle field where we find aplenty of German graves.

I am very anxious to view the outcome of the barrage of rifle bullets I dropped upon and around the ammunition cart I previously told you about. But still I cannot also but help to hold a reluctance to seeing it. My heart thumps audibly as we near the cart, the top of which we can only see before getting right upon it.

13. Crezancy

One of the fellows with me says, "Here is a German with his toes sticking out of his grave." It cannot be one of those I shot as it is yet too far removed from the cart. Looking upon the hill where we shot from, the parapet of the trench is easily visible; and it is from this point of observation that one can so easily understand why the Germans in this field had no chance against us the morning of the 15th. And had the Germans known we were entrenched up there, I very much doubt that they would have undertaken such a bold and daring chance.

Before reaching a point such that brings us in plain view of most all the cart, I discover that it is filled with bullet holes. Still closer observation reveals three German graves and one American grave. I could never imagine an excuse for the latter's grave unless he was killed while on patrol the night of the 15th. As I look upon these three enemies' graves, I do not allow my mind to run mad with the foolish idea that I committed murder in my action. While I do not relish the fact that it fell upon me to do it, I make up my mind not to let it affect me other than satisfy my mind with thoughts such that if I had not got them they would have gotten me or some of my comrades. I consider to not shoot an enemy in battle is an act of a fool only; such action being nothing less than traitorous.

Having satisfied ourselves with our adventures, we return to our quarters where I lie down and rest until the sound for chow is given.

After eating lunch, I perch myself upon a window sill in my room and watch the flares as they again shoot into the sky over the German territory; but for what purpose I nor any other American this side of the Marne knows. Yes, Red might be right; it might not all be over yet. I become more convinced it is not all over when I gather from what someone on the ground directly under my window says. He is telling some more fellows that German spies have been seen this side of the river.

Someone in the crowd says, "You mean German patrolmen don't you?"

"Maybe so," the fellow telling of the Germans says, "but they say they are spies."

Someone, maybe one of those who have been talking says, "That don't mean the Germans are quite givin' it all up."

As I Saw It in the Trenches

I reason in my own way that the Germans are trying to learn, definitely, our actions; our intentions. Following my conclusions of the Germans' actions, I sprawl upon my blanket for a little rest; and little rest I get before the cook would have sounded his midnight crow, a shrill whistle sounds loudly followed with the command to roll pack and report in the street quickly.

Assembling in the street, the Company and in fact the whole battalion moves out in the direction of the Marne to a little later be caught within the walls of blazing hell, or at least allow me to compare it with such.

14

Forced to
Lie Under Fire

German flares still decorate the elements across the river. Judging from them the enemy cannot have retreated as far as reports indicated. Even the signals cause me to feel that there is trouble ahead; and yet, I suppose, this could be due to my mental psychology.

As we hike along the road, a shell can be heard now and then burst upon the road ahead; and occasionally sparks of fire flash and pierce the darkness when the shells burst upon the hard surface. Shells can be heard more numerously further on toward the river. The Germans seem to know we are on the road judging from the bombs they are dropping upon it.

The most daring one of these steel demons is heard coming from across the Marne, passing over us and lighting so close that its shrapnel and fragments squeal and flutter through the air entirely too close by to make believe it is not out for the kill. We are again facing what we faced or rather lay under the night of the 14th; except that they are not so numerous yet as they were then.

It is now that I realize that "Red" must have known or at least made a good guess that this thing was not over yet. Recalling our conversation of night before last I make mention, as we walk along, that Red knows his stuff about this war. He, hearing me, says, "I guess you see now that I was right don't you?"

"For once you are right," I reply. "And I think it is such a pity that you could not have seen fit to prophesy in the other direction."

Another bomb jars the ground so thoroughly that either of us forget all about our useless conversation, turning our attention to that which is defying us from across the river. Another and another lights close by the roadside causing a sag in the file of men in the road. Smaller shells zipping through the air to a tenth of a second later bang upon the road or close to it. The men come to a halt for what cause I am ignorant of unless the barrage has them in check. A wounded doughboy supported by two others, one on either side, passes by, seemingly suffering intense pain.

The small shells or zip-bangs as they are called, continue feeding the road in front of where I am and our stop surely must mean that the officers are afraid to risk the lives of the men through this bombardment. A larger shell lights just to the right of the road and about thirty feet from where I stand. Behaving like a herd of stampeding cattle, we hurry further back down the road, some men falling and suffering from being stepped upon in the wild rush to move out of danger. It is not until we become kind of settled that I can hear men screaming and complaining in response to having been hit by the shrapnel or fragments of the shell. A man running down the road and stopping where we are densely congested, says, "My buddy got blowed all to pieces and a lot got wounded." His words are choked out and plainly indicative that he is much grieved at the loss of his trench pal.

"Oh, my arm! My arm!" a wounded fellow hobbling down the road says. These words attracting my attention to his arms, reveals that his left arm has almost been chopped off by a shell fragment, leaving it swinging loosely by his side as he travels hysterically down the road. Closely followed by the wounded man, a lieutenant says "Fall out by the side of the road in the ditch until you are told to move up." He continues on down the road repeating the command and everybody responds but find ourselves so congested that we have to lie partly upon one another lest a shrapnel might pierce our backs. No sooner than we are settled in the ditch, a heavy bomb lights a little to my rear in the road, shooting its shrapnel into the air and spraying us with dirt and rock. Amidst the falling dirt and stone someone is heard talking loudly. It is Captain Woodside. He tells his lieutenants to move their platoons back out of the barrage. Whistles can be heard sounding to attract the men's attention, and then the officers can be heard telling their platoons to "move back down the road."

On rising to execute orders, it seems that the road in front is a mass of geysers spouting fire into the air.

The zip-bangs are coming through aplenty up there and it seems that the speed and power they bring with them is enough to knock the road in two. The Germans send them from across the Marne in bunches in some spots and there can nothing be left living where they land.

The barrage grows more intense all the time. If we were a little further up the road we could never live to tell how it all turned out. Now and then it seems that a few bombs can be heard falling in or nearby Crezancy. In the direction of the river, it sounds like the barrage is just as intense as the night of the 14th.

We have by now withdrawn a little way back down the road and lie in the ditch again. Wounded men are being brought back in considerable numbers. Some of them complain loudly as they hobble along looking for another bomb to put the finishing touches of their chances of living through it. It is a pretty easy matter to see the men as it is not such a dark night. They swarm by moving out of the barrage that is taking so many lives up there. Some of them talk loudly as if to be excited or in a hurry. On hearing a shell approaching, they fall down in the road and then move again as soon as the shell has spent its effect.

A star shell can be seen ascending across the river. The officers scream for everybody to lie down and be still. The shell explodes at which time everything is visible as far away as if the sun were shining. It is when the luminous rays appear that I take the opportunity to see just what is happening. Men recently killed can be seen lying in the road and even some who are not yet out of the immediate range of the center of the barrage running down the road with rifle swinging in one hand and pack bouncing up and down on the back.

A flash across the river draws my attention in that direction. It is a fiery cannon that sends bombs across delivering them to us in defiance to our trying to force our way across the river. A high hill on which the flash of fire appeared stands out boldly above everything else this side of the river. It must be at least a mile by way of a straight line to the top of the hill. But the light being so luminous, one can easily see the small trees that hide its surface. It is from among these trees on top of this hill that the German batteries are feeding us with this barrage. It is no doubt that it is from this point that these small speedy one-pounder shells spring, a part of a second later banging upon the road or nearby with vociferous and bloodthirsty reports. The radiant light having disappeared, I resume my horizontal position back in the ditch to await the fatality of the barrage or whatever unknown action we are to take next.

As we lie snugged away in this ditch, gases from high explosives mixed with the odor of carrion aggravates the sense of smell causing us to even more detest any word that sounds like war. But as we lie here under as certain death as could possibly announce its approach from across the Marne, word is passed down the ditch that the bridge we were to cross the river on had been blown up and that we have to lie in wait until the engineers can get another bridge ready. This message is the first definite proof that we were to cross the river; but, morally, however, we knew we were on our way to resume our attack on the Germans which meant we had to cross over.

Now that we are to lie here until another bridge is constructed, it is certain to result in our crossing over after sunrise, at which time we will have thought we have been having a plaything of it during the night compared with crossing the Marne.

An ambulance coming up the road lands in a shell hole, rendering the vehicle inoperative and leaving the wounded still nursing their pains under the unmerciful downpour of steel-jacketed devils. A bombastic devil dives down nearby the ambulance, sending dirt and debris and no doubt shrapnel and fragments beating against the crippled machine as if to indicate that the bomb is doing it all to avenge itself for some dire wrong imposed upon it. The machine stands almost vertically upon its motor as men strive to dislodge it from the imprisonment. But such efforts are all in vain and the approach of another wild demon from across the river puts the men on the run for safety; but the bomb held one of the men's names written correctly, as he is brought down with the explosion and falling so near me that he lies visible above the ditch in the road.

The German batteries still center the barrage upon the road above us and especially further on in the direction of the river. It seems like a million blasts of dynamite are dealing down curses on mother earth up there as the barrage bangs down upon the road and nearby vicinity.

Should this barrage be dropping bombs into the river's stream, chances are that the engineers will be unable to construct the bridge as a result of which we might retire to Crezancy or at least give up the attempt to cross over. Such conclusions leaves one, or me, at least, not knowing which I would prefer as I know we will have to go over sooner or later. On the other hand, the sound of the barrage up there is enough to entice anyone not to choose going across. But which soldier is it that is granted his choice about anything to say nothing about his choice to cross or not to cross? I know I have no choice coming and as a result, have long since learned that it is up to me to make the best of that which I am sent against. Any time we might be called out of the ditch to resume the hike that will take us into those spouting geysers that are scarring the earth in a million spots up there. Flashes of light can be seen to sweep over us as fire emits from the shells that light upon the road nearby. Shrapnel can be heard fast shooting through the air with velocity sufficient to pass the steel marble through several men. Fragments buzz and flutter madly as if to be hunting a horse or man to tear open.

Someone says, "This is a terrible place to keep a bunch of men waiting for a bridge to be built. A bomb is liable to blow us all into bits before that bridge is finished."

"Yes," replies someone else, "They know our intentions and they do not intend to let us pass to the river. That is why they are centering the barrage upon the road in front of us."

The last fellow speaks just what I have been thinking for some time. And if by means of that star shell they discovered us here, the barrage will be centered on us right here within less time than it takes to change the range of their batteries. It is then we will be ground into pulverized flesh.

Looking up out of the ditch again, I can see the German batteries belching fire as they send their devastating steel over the stream to blow us all the way back to Crezancy. The small shells still squeal through the air to burst sharply, sending fragments in pursuit of prey.

Finding that gazing out of the ditch and seeing the flashes of guns and shells increases the intensity of my suspense, I resolve to lie flat upon my belly with face on my arm to cut off vision of the light. As I lie still listening to the shellfire, mostly in the vicinity of the Marne, I vividly recall the barrage the night of the 14th, when it looked impossible that a single man could come through whole. But here we are again undergoing the same thing except that the shells are not so numerous right here as then. It matters not how few the chances of living through it seem to grow, I cannot but recall the inanimate voice that directed me out of certain death that night. It is this consoling recollection that causes me to be able to endure the intensity of the unmerciful threats that the Germans throw down on us tonight.

Daylight finds us still lying in the ditch by the side of the road. The bridge is not yet finished, or at least it seems that must be the case.

The manner in which the Germans shell is different to what it was during the night. The smaller shells seem to still be falling in our surrounding vicinity while the larger ones fall in the vicinity of the river.

The Germans are sure to see us in the event we get into motion; and it is almost evident that we won't lie here all day. No indeed, for now the whistles sound for us to resume our vertical positions. It is on rising that I see the small shells throwing a dust screen over the road in front of us. It will be impossible to make it through the barrage as it rains down upon the road like a hail storm.

The road seems to be full of men as far back as Crezancy. The line of khaki-clad soldiers waves slowly in the direction of the barrage. But it cannot be possible that they will carry us through it lest we be blown into atoms. Only a few platoons hold positions in the road ahead of that of my own. Their movement will determine if we are supposed to attempt going through the shelling. A whistle sounds from a lieutenant's mouth at which time he motions his platoon, which is in front around the barrage. His actions result in a great suspense falling from our minds. The men trot around the barrage and it is when I near the point where we leave the road that shrapnel scream above my head. Nearing this point, nearly all the men bend over and choose a crouched position in traveling rather than remaining straight for fear that our heads will be cut from our shoulders.

15

Crossing the Marne

It is through misfortune and emergency that we proceed under shell- fire to the river where we will attempt to cross it. It means far more sacrifice of lives than if we could have crossed over during darkness. But now as we fast hike along, a man now and then is brought down either by a fragment or shrapnel bullet or both. The shelling becomes more intense the further we go and at times it becomes necessary again to leave the road to trick the intention of falling shells in same.

Nearing the river, it becomes evident that the road and near vicinity have undergone a powerful siege of shelling. The carcasses of the dead horses have been struck by shell, tearing them to pieces and increasing the rotten odor that almost stifles us. The road is a horrible sight, being so badly torn that it is a hard matter to get over it afoot to say nothing of traffic.

Airplanes are now exploring our side of the river, hovering so low down that the air disturbed by the wings almost shoves us down. The tops of trees in front of us bow as if intending to fall as the planes roar above their tops.

A squadron of German planes roaring madly from across the river drop bombs, scattering them along near the men, doing everything possible to check them before they cross over. Pretty soon another squadron flies over and the earth quakes under the barrage of serial bombs as they bang toward us spouting smoke and dirt in the air, raining them down upon us as though it were hailstones beating down upon our helmets.

The group shows that it has gone through another terrible barrage. It seems that the Germans must have thought that the Americans were trying to cross over last night judging from the amount of shelling that went on here during the night. They still shell immensely and as they fall among the trees the shrapnel and fragments cut limbs and leaves from the trees screening the ground with a layer of green.

The men in front are put into confusion when a bomb falls among them, killing several and wounding even more. The wounded who can walk hurry to the rear, some of them bleeding from face and hands while others show no signs of wounds except from facial expressions or from complaints. The men hop over the dead to hurry themselves to the river lest they are blown to pieces.

Coming in sight of the river's bank, it seems that the German batteries are centering the shelling there. Smoke shoots high in the air at the explosions of each shell. Water can be seen spurting above the bank which is evidence that some bombs are falling in the stream. And if the bridge should again be blown up, God only knows what will become of all the men caught here at the mercy of the unmerciful enemy.

Parts of bricks lie in the road among the stone and other debris of the houses of the small town that stood here before barrage. Not a house now stands as it is plain that every building has been beaten down to the ground pillow.

Coming in view of the stream reveals a pontoon bridge that we will cross over on. Men cross over, all the time in a rush, seemingly to try and beat a bomb to their destination.

Captain Woodside gestures his Company around some dropping shells that fall directly in our front. It is about this time that I hear him yell, "Get out of that hole and get your men ready to cross over." I find that it is one of the sergeants he is talking to, the same sergeant that snarled at the dead Frenchman I told you about. The sergeant says "I am shell shocked."

"Shell shocked, hell," the captain yells out. "You are scared to death." At this description, the sergeant jumps from the hole he was in, but in response to another shell that lands nearby, springs back into the hole, bobbing up and down at the explosion of each shell, which are too plenty.

Shrapnel scream above our heads when a shell lands right in front of me. This time I bring myself upon the ground with the belief that I must assuredly be hit now; for I suppose I got my idea from being thumped with clots of dirt. Dirt rains down upon us as we lie sprawled upon the ground waiting for the next one to put an end to all of it. Turning my head, I see the captain resting on his all fours looking towards the bridge, seemingly, waiting for it to become clear so that he can command his men to cross. Glancing at the bridge myself, I see a man fall into the water from being hit by a machine gun bullet for it is by now that I notice the water at the bridge being kicked up by bullets. A machine-gun can be heard upon the hill across the river chattering away, dropping bullets in the river and killing and wounding everyone possible as the men try to cross. They defy our attempt to cross from every angle. They use artillery, machine-guns and aeroplanes; and might result in their using rifles and bayonets.

The men that cross safely hurry downside the river to conceal themselves behind high steep inclines of the hill. Every man seems to be full of excitement from the machine-guns and artillery that bang and pepper the water in mad effort to reach us. Another man falls from the bridge to be taken down, never to rise again. The machine-gun cackles more audibly than ever, peppering the water and bridge like a shower of hail. Men cross in intervals of about eight feet.

A large shell landing in the edge of the water at the closest point to us shoots the water into the air and raining down upon as though a shower of rain was falling. A shell that falls into the river nearby the bridge almost breaks it in two as the large waves caused by the bomb's disturbance shakes it so severely that the men on it fall into the river to only save themselves by holding on until the water becomes more civil. The men on the bank are held in great suspense for the fate of the unfortunate men that struggle to gain footing and cross under the barrage of machine-gun bullets that rain down upon the bridge. It is through all these attractions that I happen to notice that the bridge sags below the surface of the water in places. This is due to the bullets piercing the pontoons that support the bridge.

It coming our time to cross the river, the captain orders the first platoon across. The lieutenants and sergeants standing at the edge of the bridge, direct the men as to the intervals to take in crossing. At last our Company executes the much-dreaded task and in a way a heavy suspense is being removed from our shoulders to know that we might, in a few minutes, have succeeded in doing that which many of us thought almost impossible in the daytime. The machine-gun up there still continues its contempt, however, and is resulting in some of the men being felled from the bridge either wounded or dead. The badly wounded flounder around in the water helplessly trying to save themselves from certain death from drowning. The machine-gun has no mercy, however, and continues to spit down bullets to kill every man that tries to cross.

I hear the captain yell out to the men to speed it up. It is impossible for the men to run fast, for as they attempt it the bridge vibrates up and down so much that the men cannot travel at all.

It coming my platoon's time to cross over, I am terribly sponsored by the nervous tension that inspires me to act quickly and get it over with. And Oh! If I were only on the other side of the river what a relief it would be even though the chances of living over there are not so many. Only two squads are to cross ahead of my own. Squad One" getting on the bridge, Squad "Two" takes up the attempt. Now Squad "Three" gets on the move and it is as we move toward the bridge that I see a man pitch off into the stream and grab the bridge through effort to save his life. Moving on the bridge, I can more easily discern that the bullets are peppering down upon it by the hundreds. The planks are filled with bullet holes. Covering about half the distance of the bridge, I find that the wounded man is losing his hold and is being carried under by the swiftly moving stream. On his way down to the river's bottom, he leaves a stream of blubbers trickling towards the surface of the water. The water being so clear, one can see all the way to the bottom of the river. There, men killed in their attempt to cross, lie humped or stretched to never see the other side of the Marne or the other side of the ocean. "Thank God," are my words on reaching the other side of the river. On reaching the bank, a German airman flies low over the stream, his machine-gun chattering and the bullets zipping by, eager to add some prey to its crew. Realizing that the danger is not by all means over yet, I run behind an old broken-off pillow of a demolished building to protect myself. Discovering that the plane is circling, I make sure that its actions are in response to trying to get me. So I closely hug and circle the pillow keeping it between the plane and me. The plane soaring out of danger, I resume running with the rest of those who had been lying flat upon their bellies in response to the plane's activities.

15. Crossing the Marne

A few minutes after I cross, all the Company save its several losses have made it across and are moving up the river to take positions. The captain comes running along behind the last men to cross and quarreling at a sergeant who has not been doing to suit him.

This climaxing the crossing of the Marne, the stream no longer separates the Company and its enemy.

16

Witnessing the Aerial Fights

Shells still rain down the other side of the river. On this side, it is most impossible for any to fall as the hillside's incline is so nearly vertical that they fall either in or the other side of the stream. Men subjected to shellfire run here and thither to evade the detriments of approaching shells.

Men still continue to give up to the hungry stream as machine-gun bullets pour down upon the bridge. The chatter of the gun can be heard above the roaring in my head caused by the exploding bombs. For a second the gun stops to resume with a volley of bullets that whistle down into the water and on the bridge, hungry to take the lives of the men, sending them down into river's bottom where they are sure never to again defy the German Kaiser. The river seems to be hungry for the khaki uniforms as its water swiftly moves down gulping them as though they were destined to its charms.

Even though the men on this side feel reasonably sure we are out of danger of the tormenting shells, we cannot help but pull ourselves towards the ground as they scream over the steep incline to bang down upon the water or opposite bank. While relief hovers over my mind and joy is carried through my veins from having crossed over safely, I cannot help but be thrilled as I watch the shells fight the efforts of the Americans to cross the river. It is indeed an uncomfortable thrill to watch all this and especially is it a thrill in one incident when a man is swept down upon his back by the vacuum of a shell that passes too close to his person. I can imagine the leather strap that holds his helmet in place choking him when his steel hat naturally is inclined to be torn from his head.

16. Witnessing the Aerial Flights

The man lies quietly for a few seconds trying to grab his faculties together to determine whether he is killed or not. On responding to the knowledge of good fortune, he jumps up and runs down next to the water, fumbling with his pack as though it had been uncomfortably misplaced during his surprising and unconscious moments.

Another thrill that draws our attentions in a different direction is the roaring of two aeroplanes that stage a fight above the hill. The machine-guns chatter from the planes in defiance to each other's enemy. The planes dart under and over each other like two birds staging a fight in the air. One of them is a German plane and the other an American plane. The large black crosses under the German plane become conspicuous when the plane turns a somersault to renew its attack upon its enemy. I look for them to collide; but I suppose they are too skilled with their machinery for such a thing to happen. The machine-guns clatter madly trying to bring down either's prey before it is brought down as prey itself. The German plane resuming a natural position, struts fast away across the river while the American plane roars its victorious growl in boasting fashion above the hill. The German plane was only fooling it seems, as it turns back to resume the fight against the cocky American machine. I take it that it must have flown away to give the operator of the gun time to reload or maneuver with the gun in some way. As the machine charges back from across the river, it opens up on its antagonist with a swarm of bullets that meet an unwelcome reception with the return of a barrage of steel hornets that sink their stings into the German machine trying to bring it down before their own nest is lowered into the trees below. The machines taking various positions in their engagements with each other, result in bullets sweeping the air and ground from many angles. Frequently a flurry of bullets can be heard and seen kicking up dirt as they sweep upon the ground like large drops of summer rain. It is when a flurry of them passes among a few of us that we all take horizontal positions, covering our heads well with our steel helmets. The drops of raining steel having passed by and hearing someone say, "Oh! I'm hit!" I look around to find that one of the men has been hit in the leg with one of the bullets. As the victim perches upon his haunches squeezing his wound and indicating pain or fright or both with an unusual display of facial horror, I cannot help but say in my own silent manner, "You lucky fool! Just to think you will soon be resting upon a bed all the way out of this earth of hells but still you haven't any more sense than to grieve over your good fortune." In another second's time I look back to witness the serial encounter, and about the same time discover that the American plane is taking a nose dive toward to the earth. I think at first the aviator's action might be some act of strategy to elude the German airman but a moment later reveals that the action meant fatality for the American as the plane crashes upon the ground, leaving the German birdman flying safely away while the plane itself seems to strut away with boastful gratification. The victorious aviator has not flown completely away as we thought, however. He returns once more to belittle us by turning loops directly over the river and then sailing upside down until lost to view over the tops of the tree upon the hill.

Our eyes shine with curiosity to run upon the hillside and view the dead man and wreckage of the plane but the German machine-gunners keep too close a vigil over the point where it fell to venture out into such a fatal risk. Hence, it is our common sense reasoning that prompts us to remain and evade being put on the spot by our natural inclinations.

The Americans still feed the hungry Marne in their crossing over. I notice that men cross over about two hundred yards above. They also cross on a pontoon bridge and no doubt some of them give feed to the river as they try to conquer its water. A machine-gun can be heard upon the hill directly across from this bridge and it's a sure thing that the clatter of the gun is due to its spitting bullets down upon the men while they attempt to execute the command to cross. As men from both bridges make it across, they seek protection from machine-guns and bombs at the foot of the hill. Some takeup breast-works behind the large stones while most of them sprawl upon the ground to await further orders.

While we lie in wait for orders to attack the machine-guns up on the hill, which I understand we are to do, I, as nervous and uncertain about it all as I am, witness with some kick those things you are reading about in this Chapter. The reason I am able to set aside a chapter on "Aerial Combats" at this time is due to it having happened that several aerial engagements took place while we lay in suspense until the amount of men sufficient to carry on an attack crossed over. No doubt you have read or at least know that Quentin Roosevelt was killed in an aerial encounter. I am not certain that I saw his plane in action; however, it is known that he was brought down on this same front which is in the vicinity of Reims.

It seems that the enemy has done everything consistent in trying to put a stop to our pursuit of them. Last night our bridge was blown up; today our men die from shellfire and those nasty steel yellow jackets that swarm down upon us having no mercy, but on the other hand the cruel courage to pierce us to the core and deliver us to the greedy Marne to forever and eternity be swallowed up and rot beneath its clear waters. So do those beasts of prey mercilessly swoop down on us to carry away some of the men in the form of mangled flesh.

Above an enemy plane soars among some scattering clouds. It behaves as though it were suspended from the sky by means of a cord. Black wads of smoke begin to appear close by it. The plane seeks a still higher altitude. The anti-aircraft guns continue to shell it as it gets higher. After three balls of smoke have appeared near the plane, the report of the first clucks in our ears; then the second; then the third and on in succession several breaths after the plane nose-dives as if being brought down; the plane only fools, dropping several hundred feet, it regains its flying position and sails away to protection while the smoke balls, maybe from a different source, appear in spontaneous succession in their pursuit of the beast of prey.

We crouch lazily back on our packs, the excitement having disappeared. Fragments buzz and hiss in their descent to the earth. They can be heard stripping the leaves from the trees as they drop into the woods a little above us.

Something moves under my underwear with their "make yourself at home steps." It crawls across my belly that is now far less in circumference than when I first entered this land of craters. I unbutton my trousers, hoist my shirt tail, unbutton my underwear and not to my surprise find a nice white, four-legged black-spined Heine roosting among my hairs with the expressed attitude that I had invited him over for a long stay. But it means nothing but fatality to the proud cootie. He dies a cruel death between my thumbnail and the stock of my rifle.

As I Saw It in the Trenches

I again slump back upon my pack to feel for the footsteps of some more unwelcome hosts. My attention is interrupted by a boy that lies close to me sniffing his nose and choking: indications of heavy crosses. He chokes out a few words to a fellow nearer him than I. His emotions bring me to inquisitive listening. I learn through a few words that he is grieved over his "buddy" having been into atoms by a bomb the other side of the Marne. Yes, the heavy-hearted fellow's name is Pendleton. It is the first time a lump forms in my throat.

Planes hum again in the air over us: Four of them. Three enemy planes; one American plane. Among the loud roars of the planes, machine-guns can be heard rattling: three German planes behind; one American plane ahead. An aerial race is on. It is exciting to see them trying to seek a spied record up there; or should I say a speed record. It certainly cannot be what these enemies are out for. It is each other's altitude they seek to shorten; shorten all the way to the zero mark. The American understands that he cannot hope to stay aloft against such superior number of enemies, for now two more enemy planes soar into the scene. It is now that the American becomes more concerned than previously about making his getaway. The hum of the plane becomes more audible in volume. The German planes come closer; closer in pursuit. They slowly decrease the distance between their planes and the American's. Machine-guns bark more vociferously; the American plane darts down and up like a hawk being chased by a martin. The enemy's planes close in closer; one German plane lifts his altitude and hovers over the American's. The German aviator drops bullets down upon the back of the American birdmen as if a storm of hail were beating down upon his plane. The German airmen know the victory belongs to them for three of the planes have quit the chase and gone in another direction for additional prey. One stays in close behind the American. A screen of smoke appears in the air behind the helpless American's plane. The smoke seems to be shooting out the tail of the machine. A second longer and the tail of the plane cannot be seen; it is too completely wrapped in smoke. A second more and the smoke is displaced by a mass of flames that lap hungrily behind the doomed plane. Someone says "Look, something is falling from the plane." Everyone gazes with excited eyes. "A man," another says. The flames become too intense. The aviator chooses to jump from the plane rather than burning alive in the air. He leaps from the plane and crushes his body upon the hard surfaces of the earth. And as someone said afterwards, "Maybe he was trying to jump into the river." True it could have been but certain death would have been the only result had he fallen in the water. The plane sails on unmanned across the river. Instantaneously, the flames whip above the whole machine. The plane comes motor first to the earth, crashing into the wooded section over there. Flames leap above the treetops lapping at the sky and reaching with hungrier fingers that seem to be trying to drag something in among the trees that is more reliable than the trees themselves.

An hour later, the fire has ceased for the greater part. The river and its opposite bank are not the center of blazing geysers that they were at the time I have supposed to have been writing above. Now and then a bomb swishes across the river; now and then one falls in the river above that causes the stream to take on the ugly appearance it had more than an hour ago; most all the men seem to be across that intend to cross over; the machine-guns are more reticent; only every now and then they give a few whines to keep in trim. Indeed, most all the earthly activities seem to have given back to be entertained by the series of serial stunts. In response to a bold bomb that whines directly above, we again occupy the position one ordinarily occupies during a lengthy prayer.

More than another hour passes. Meanwhile, the officers, and in particular the Company Commander, have been maneuvering some definite strategies by which to attack the machine-guns upon the hill. The machine-guns keep silent. Their guns are cooling off. The Germans up there know that we mean to attack. They know we have to attack or else say we are afraid to. "Not all the machine-guns have been in operation that are up there," someone remarks. Guess he might be right. I'll bet they are just fooling us to draw us into the most certain circle of death that has confronted us yet. They sit nested in the brush and grass up there and hidden behind a breast-work of piled-up stone with the muzzle of the gun peeking out through the opening of a missing stone. They will send a flurry of steel beans at us when the time is ripe. Won't it be hell! We will bow before the guns and their operators as if we were bowing before the old Emperor Kaiser himself. Ha! The Heinies are no fools.

They know strategy. They pull their main body of men back in safety but still leading us to believe they are in the front line ready to gore us to the core with the white steel that clicks and glitters through the bushes, trees, wire entanglements through No-Man's land and into the khaki uniforms and then into the flesh and bones of the over-sea enemy. While we might be looking on the level surface for the grey enemy, reports similar to those of a thousand bursting Roman candles might pierce the leaves, limbs and moss of a tree to be followed by ten thousand bullets that are known to mow men to the ground as if so many stalks of what were being felled by a mowing machine. Red is no longer by himself with respect to nursing the conceivable string of fates that are sure to tag many of those who attempt to advance upon the furrow-faced enemy; the faces so mis-figured by too many days and nights of the merciless toil out here. I myself have begun to hibernate these horrid conceptions. And these are the conceivable that entertain my mind as I, here, lie in wait for the command to ascend the hill.

My burdensome mind is suddenly interrupted when several fellows gesture their whole bodies in response to hearing some aeroplanes that come snorting down the river closely hovering the water with their wide, outstretched wings. A bombing squadron of planes. No mistake about that. No. No. No mistake. They are bombing planes and they are enemy planes too. Five of them in all; three in the lead; two that follow up. They roar over us. They fan us with their prominent wings; the very vibrations of the powerful motors almost drive our eardrums all the way into our brain. What do they care if they do? It is the bridges and us they are out to destroy.

They drop bombs in the river. The bridges behave madly from the effects of the swirling water. The bombs again have the stream giving up its water to the air. The water spurts high into the air when the serial beast drops into the stream. Boom! Boom! The river opens up its bosom to the unwelcome hosts. The air soon becomes full of vapor and mist. The sun shines brightly and thus a rainbow shapes itself over the water, the trees in the background acting as a silhouette. The bridge below, the one my Company used in crossing, rises with the disturbed waves having the appearance of a large whale that rises above the surface on the sea. The pressure and strain are too great. The bridge breaks in the middle, each half swings fast around to a few seconds later lie parallel with the bank that holds it.

The bridge above floats in safety. It still rocks a little but the river current is fast destroying the effect of the surging waves, thus bringing the bridge back to its normal stillness. The planes disappear in the distant horizon. The men in the machines can easily be imagined roaring deep haw! Haw, haws as their victorious planes spirit them away to report their fruitful efforts.

Our serial thrills are suddenly ended. The Company Commander orders us to make ready for the attack we will soon carry against the machine-guns. Our hearts thump loudly. Our veins pulsate at the thought of having to engage that nest of fiery devils that a few hours ago left so many wallowing in the Marne's bottom. It was not complete then. We must give them a chance to complete their desire. We must all get killed today. But what if we do? There are others to take our places. Yes, others to take our places here on the front but no one can take our places in the loved one's hearts across that blue salty brine. This is war. This is war. Here goes.

17

The Machine-Gun
Engagements

Somewhere in the distance the enemy observes our positions. Those upon the hill know them already. They watch for us. They expect us. They know our intentions. They know we will attack sometime. Maybe not today but sometime. Today it is a movement of war on our part. The Germans do not move more than raising their arms and hands in preparation to shoot our heads off. They sneak behind objects and then when we attack they attack with their guns spitting steel and fire bringing us down as if we're ordinary fowls or beasts of valueless ownership.

As we move through the woods, I hear a crack and looking around I see a tall black mustached figure up in a tree. A German rolls out of the tree and bumps the ground loudly. Noticing that the fellow, whose name is Nutson, continues walking around the tree and quarrelling about something, I look up into the tree and find another German trying to protect himself behind the trunk of the tree from Nutson. The German mumbles words that we cannot understand. We know, however, that he begs Nutson not to kill him. To furnish a little comedy, Nutson yells, "Scare him around so I can get a shot at him." He then sights and fires. The German quivers, breaks his hold and tumbles out upon the ground. Their machine-gun still remains in the tree fastened to limbs. This is the last excitement before reaching the outskirts of the woods next to the field.

We respond to the orders of the captain. We balance ourselves upon our feet. Our faces are furrowed with disgust and exposure. Red's eyes, face and nose shows the effects of trench life. His eyes are red and lifeless-looking; his face is red and flushed, not from the result of good old vigor but from loss of sleep and mental agony. He mutters, "Ah hell!" as he slings his pack across his back, adjusting the supporting straps. Sergeant Easterday stands there all supported on his broom handle legs. I should think he would hesitate to risk his body and pack out on them. He is not, however, and when we settle down for the night if we are struck down by the enemy, the sergeant will be there. This goes to show you how good his tiny legs are. "Well Sarge," I say. "Guess we will meet beyond the clouds before darkness overtakes us. Is that the way you feel about it?"

Seemingly not very moved by what I saw or by the outcome of the hell up there, he drags a slow smile across his lips and replies, "Maybe."

Sergeant Vogt, a typical blond man and to my opinion not a fit subject to be a sergeant out here on the front, turns to me and says, "You must be yellow. I intend to get at least ten of them today." His last words find his eyes dragging from off my face.

"I might get as many as you, sergeant, and we will just wait and see who it is that is afraid up here on this front," I reply.

Corporal Dublinsky, of most overbearing qualities, joins the argument by saying, "I have never seen a conscript yet that was worth a damn on the front lines." Before I have time to remind him that I have already three notches on my rifle stock to his doubtless one, Lieutenant Fry interrupts by storming at the corporal to "shut up."

With packs adjusted, helmets strapped to our heads, gas masks at the "alert" and bayonets flickering sunny reflections upon the ground and upon one another of the men, we begin ascending the hill. Some of us will fall where we will die and from where we will be carried away to the hospital.

Machine-guns began to rattle up there. They know we are on our way. We keep low and hug the hill in our crawl up it. Bullets zip and hiss above our heads. I keep my helmet well in line of the passing steel. Our packs soon grow heavy, our backs twitch and almost scream under the heavy burden of body and pack. Our hearts beat loudly against our chests. Our throats begin to parch; they are moistened by a swallow of water. Our breath swishes out through our mouths. Our legs fail under the heavy load. They have grown wobbly under such strain. The hill is so nearly vertical that it is impossible to be helped along by the momentum of the body. It is under the strain of every muscle in the body that we move an inch. Our faces glow with redness. Sweat beads pop out all over our heads and faces; the large drops become restless and flow down our countenances assembling on our chins and emptying off on our blouse fronts to saturate it all the way to our belts. Our underwear soon becomes saturated; our whole body takes on a stinging sensation due to the woolen underwear. Our little sacred pets soon become uncomfortable and begin to crawl from place to place. I wish mine would behave. I have too many antagonists already.

The grueling grind upward results in complete exhaustion with some of us. I am overcome with too heavy strain and loss of strength. I flop behind a stone that protrudes out of the ground. Bullets are now cutting the air close above me. Red lies five feet to my right and a little in front. His face is as red as a rose. I believe the blood will break through the skin. His red mustache twitches. He groans. He puffs. He swears. He lays his face flat on the ground. I hear him say, "I can't go any further." I cannot help but sympathize with him. He is not a bad sort; just a fellow who gripes at almost anything. But here he has splendid excuses for griping. We all have good excuses and we use them. Even the officers who, of course, one expects to be the last to complain, indicate pain and suffering upon their faces. A lieutenant trudges slowly forward as he pulls himself along by means of protruding stones. All the men move like snails. They cannot move otherwise.

I can hear my blood swish at each heartbeat. How can we attack when it is impossible to reach the enemy for the unconquerable barrier that fights our efforts? It is too great for man's power to conquer in a hurry. It must be done gradually. It means intervals of rest for those who fight the grassy and vertical wall of this stony baby mountain.

Machine-guns have taken up a stiffer fight of resistance. I hear more and more echoes beating against the leaves and trees. More bullets zip by. They can be heard to strike stones and then whine through the air. It all means they are getting our levels. They are beginning to see us. It won't be long now.

Lieutenant Fry's helmet connects with a bullet. He rolls a little way back down the hill. He grabs a stone and supports himself. The bullet has already whined through the air. The officer seems somewhat excited. Blood streams down his face. He unstraps his helmet and removes it from his head. Blood now slushes down his face, completely blinding him. The bullet deeply grooves his steel helmet in front, cutting his scalp all the way to the skull. His hair is a mass of clotted blood. The Company commander has already learned that he is wounded and has ordered him to report back at the dressing station. He scrambles back down the hill leaving his platoon in charge of a sergeant. The sergeant's name is Vohn.

The fire up there ceases. Bullets cease whistling. Again it cackles. Again the air breathes with hisses. A man rolls down the hill beating his head against stones in his descent to the foot of the hill. He is dead. A bullet plugged him. To the right upon the hill a machine-gun rattles. A new report. A surprise. Another clucks further back. The one to the right up there continues its barrage madly. A shell screams from across the river. It bangs down upon the top of the hill. It is our shell. Fragments pierce the air. The machine-gun is silenced for awhile. It reports back again, to be answered with another of our steel demons. It hushes and not again do I hear it challenge us up the hill. They are doing everything consistent to stop us. The trouble we have in ascending the hill together with the steel beads they spit down upon us should do the work. A short rest to catch our wind and we get on the move again. We will be up there after awhile or else lying at the foot of the hill dead.

The side of the hill is decorated with khaki uniforms. They move on slowly; a hump on the back and an iron stick in the other. Maybe a few of the sticks will have a chance to light their end and smack sparks at the enemy. We breathe loudly as the strain becomes more unbearable upon our weakened bodies. My sides feel that they will crack under the heavy pull. My spine hurts; my legs ache; the heavy pack has stretched my neck veins out of shape. The effects of my unfortunate experience the morning of the 15th is easily telling on me. I grit my teeth in putting everything I have into my determination to reach the top with the rest of those that will be there. A series of rests to relax my muscles and remove the ache from them are necessary for me to make it up there.

At last, through Providence and good Fortune, I reach the point where the steep incline begins to give way to the plateau. I sprawl out upon the ground behind a stone. We are near the edge of the swamp that hovers over the hill and machine-gun nests up there. Bullets whistle above; they almost hit me. Leaves fall from the trees out there as the baby demons finger through the bushes and trees in search of a juicy steak to add to the grates in the pits of old Satan's hell. The men dare not venture any further lest they get picked off. The trees and underbrush continue to deliver up the report of the guns back in the swamp just a little ways.

I hear someone say, "There is a German."

Someone else hollers, "Shoot him." Behind a small patch of scrubby bushes, a stack of rough stones protect and conceal a young German boy. He looks to be about seventeen years old. He leans lazily back against his gun, apparently with no intention of trying to kill anyone. He knows he has already killed too many on the bridge to try to act any more greedy. I change my position a little and then am able to see the kid slumped back with his hands above his head. Some two or three fellows nearer than I make him stand up and gesture him forward. The German slumps toward the ground when a swarm of bullets from his own guns back in the swamp zip above him. A boy behind me strikes me on my foot and looking around, I find that he wants a match. I pitch him the match, at which time his face drops abruptly upon the ground. The match lies untouched before him; the man quivers; blood spurts from his temple to clot under his own head. Thus, he eats the blood of death; his own blood.

The German youth motions to his thigh. He cannot respond to the command of his captors. A chain holds his thigh connecting it and the gun. I have heard such stories and now I witness one of them. The men crawl on their bellies until in reach of him. It is with much work that they finally free him of his imprisonment. The German is motioned to the rear. He responds but is suddenly interrupted by one of his own shells that squeal through the trees, lights close to him, almost tearing his arm from his shoulder. Blood soon crimsons his sleeve and side. He staggers against a tree; grows paler and paler. We that see him watch him in anxiety. He does not holler or indicate by screams that he is seriously hurt. He is just slowly bleeding to death; that is all there is to it.

The fragments from the shell fly harmlessly above us. Dirt rains down upon us. Again my head is set to roaring as if a drum were beating inside it.

German machine-guns can be heard barking further back into the woods. American batteries drop bombs in the swamp to help us bear the slaughter points we will have to engage in the woods. Sometime a gun is silenced by a French or an American bomb.

The machine-gun so close out there will deal out plenty of misery in the event we try to take it. To take it is the order, however, and it must be done. We are disciplined not to ever think of giving up pursuit or to turn back. A lot of good it would do us should we attempt to turn back.

Another bomb drops nearby where the report of the machine-gun seems to be shooting. The gun is silenced for awhile. It opens up again. Again a bomb explodes sharply back a short distance in the direction of the German sniper. Again the machine is hushed. Undoubtedly there has been ordered a few bombs in this section of the woods. Let us pray that our batteries know what to do for to breast those machine works without a few being blown all the way back to Germany would be only committing suicide.

Lieutenant Singletary crawls low among the men that lie pinned to the ground. He gestures and talks to the men but yet I cannot hear what he says. His eyes indicate that he means that something must be done. Someone says, "Flank 'em."

"Flank them," think I. "What do they mean?" I say to Corporal Simpson, who lies near me.

"I don't know just yet," he replies.

The lieutenant draws nearer. He says, "Men, we can't take this coolly like this. We must draw his attention in a single direction and flank him from a different one."

Our attention being so attracted by his instructions, some of us unconsciously support ourselves upon our hands, becoming a little too careless in the presence of a German machine-gun sniper. A few bullets pass a few feet above our heads. The officer says, "Keep low, men. Keep low, men." He continues dealing out his instructions. "We must take this nest and continue on. This baby can't keep us in check here all day. To take him, we must keep up a fire in front. We must feed him on plenty of steel and make him think we are fighting strictly from the front. Then we must——"

Right here the officer is interrupted by bullets that fly over again, "We must——lie down, men, I tell you, before some of you get picked off," he storms.

He continues, "We must literally cut these trees down with a barrage of rifle bullets while another squadron of men attack from the side."

The lieutenant has never been the man to say "You must do this and that." He always includes himself and means it.

All this time the officer has been talking he has been sitting upon a stone not thinking of protection for himself but only for his men all the time. He orders three at a time to shoot in intervals. "Do not let this baby rest. Feed him plenty of steel and never let his mouth get empty," he says. About this time, several bullets hiss close above the lieuy's head, at which time he flops quickly behind the stone he sat on and says, "I guess it's time I was getting down too."

Several of us chuckle at the lieutenant's sincerity of our protection and his absent-mindedness of his own. But believe me, that is just the sort of officer that is needed up here in this forest where on the limb of every tree death sits hungry and waiting.

The excitement kind of passing over, the officer says, "Now, I will go back and arrange things for the attack. You start shooting in about a minute's time."

The officer having gotten out of hearing, Red slowly turns his face in the direction, then looks at me and says, "Draw attention me eye; they want us to draw that machine-gun off them so they won't be worried with them bullets zipping over them."

"Do you reckon?" I say laughingly.

"Hell! yes that's it," he replies, "and you will find out I am right too."

"You are always right, Red," I answer.

Red does not make any reply as he is so sure he is always right, himself. He only twitches his red mustache and displays his upper teeth by wiping his gums with his upper lip through displaying that gripey, disgusted snarl.

We open fire as ordered. Leaves fall fast adding another green layer of leaves and twigs over the ground that is already curtained with them.

It really seems as much like war as anyone could imagine. The machine-gun hushes. No doubt it has received a surprise. It does not stay hushed. It only rests a few minutes and opens up again. We only locate ourselves better for the gunner. Now bullets fall among us. Red scoots back down a small bluff until he is well hidden behind a few fairly large stones. I can imagine him saying, "I told you so."

Bullets kick up dirt close to my left. They whistle close by and directly over my head. I look to take hiding and protection behind the stone I was behind. Someone else already occupies it. Next thought is to scoot back down the bluff as Red did until I reach a point where the bullets cannot hit me. Executing my idea I find in the action that my sides and legs are very sore. Having reached a point of safety, I again open fire sending bullets zipping through the leaves to pass far above the sniper's head unless he is perched up in a tree, which is not at all improbable.

A small black-headed boy rolls down the bluff and stops close to me. He grabs his foot and frowns frantically. "Oh! Hell! They got me at last," he cries.

It makes me want to laugh. "Got me." I was led to believe that "Got me" meant that one was killed and those were about the only two words left to say before death hooked him. A bullet only hooked him in the big toe, it reveals when he removes his shoe. The lucky guy.

A half hour later a barrage of rifle fire opens up a short distance across the swamp. The machine-gun is hushed. I listen for the report again. It stays hushed. Someone can be heard running through the bushes. He comes closer. My heart thumps as the object draws nearer. "Can it be a body of Germans?" I ask myself. No, it cannot be a whole bunch of Germans, for I only hear the footfalls of one person. Bushes beat upon each other as the being presses his way through them. I press my rifle to my shoulder preparatory to shooting the life out of whoever shows himself outside those bushes. I know it cannot be an American for an American wouldn't be coming from that direction. That is the enemy's direction. The bushes misbehave still close by. We will know in a few seconds. I can see the bushes moving. I see a hand push one aside. The person, be it German or what, is coming closer. He is penetrating the underbrush directly in my direction. Something happens that I just cannot mash the trigger. A red object appears above a bush. It is a German cap. He does not wear his helmet. He does not hold a rifle or anything in his hands. He undoubtedly does not mean to harm anyone. I know I have the advantage; therefore, I move so that he can see me for by now the German is in plain view. Seeing me he throws his hand over his head and yells, "Camerad." He runs to me and says something that, of course, I do not comprehend. I search his pockets only finding a cartridge container, part of a package of cigarettes, and an old letter. Throwing the cartridge container away, I return his cigarettes, motion him to the wounded German by the tree where they both sit and talk for a few minutes.

Men begin to rise and stir. Something has happened. A German soldier walks fast in front of an American doughboy with his hands still above his head. He hops over stones in excited behavior. A lieutenant motions the man into the woods. Surely the machine-gun nest has been destroyed. Men talk and laugh from being out of heavy suspense that they might have to openly engage the gun.

Sure thing, the machine-gun nest has been destroyed and we are unhampered to advance undisturbed. How far we don't know. Maybe fifty yards; maybe a mile. Not a mile for machine-guns can easily be heard barking less than a mile away. Maybe we are being drawn right into the muzzles of the coolie's rifles. We won't know until we get there and neither will we be in the war lying upon our bellies wishing it to end.

Maybe the strategy used in destroying this nest will work when we come upon the next. If only we knew what confronts us the remainder of the day, we could prepare in advance. Here, however, we are given no breaks. It is left for us to do as best we can under sudden surprise.

German shell-proof dugouts begin to appear among the trees and bushes. They are huge in most cases and safe from all but the heaviest shells. Lieutenant Singletary becomes handy again by taking it on himself and a few men to raid the dugouts for the Heinies. He gives the dugout-men a break by yelling "Outside!" at every dugout he finds. Maybe the enemy do not understand what he says, but they should at least know that he does not mean for them to remain in the dugout.

No Germans from the first dugout respond to the command "Outside!" and so the Lieutenant lets go a hand grenade into the opening and withdraws until the explosion occurs. Dirt and smoke roar from the opening like the smoke from a moving locomotive. If any Germans were in there alive, they are dead now. Another large dugout is nearby. The officer carries on the same routine and in response to the command "Outside!" two burly Germans appear at the opening to give themselves up. Slinging a grenade into the dugout, the lieutenant continues on through the underbrush where he is lost to me for awhile.

An hour later we are to be found lying under trees bordering a dim dirt road. Most everyone talks of his experiences of the day. Most of them discuss the difficulty they had in getting up the hill. Red still looks his contempt of it all. And he is not any too reticent about it all, either.

A lot of the men are suffering from diarrhea, dysentery and other bowel complaints. They visit distant quarters frequently and they can be heard reporting from all directions.

A runner boy runs up to the Company Commander and hands him a note. Having read it, the captain orders us to get moving. We can still hear machine-guns clattering back in the woods. Someone says, "I hope we don't have to go in that direction." But, contrary to his wishes, we move in the direction of the rattling guns and soon the distance between the guns and us grows so short that the guns report with a clear chatter instead of a dull one.

Before we know what happened or before we thought of such a thing happening, a bomb lights among us. Shrapnel pass so close to my head that I know I must be hit this time. A splinter chops Corporal Simpson's arm off below his elbow. He becomes hysterical and runs into a lieutenant's arms yelling, "I am hit." "I am hit." The lieutenant quickly examining the corporal's arm, procures a handkerchief and ties it tightly around the wounded man's arm. Blood spouting from the wound like water from a leak in a pipe soon finds the lieutenant's uniform a hideous crimson. The victim is rushed to the rear. His cries are hushed by distance.

More bombs bang down close by. The lieutenant pulls us from under fire. But it is too late so far as another man is concerned for he lies, now, dying like a hog that has been stuck by a knife. He asks for help but no one heeds his calls and hence, he is left to die. The last thing

I hear him say is, "Take me from under this shellfire so I can die like any other man." A shell falls so close by again that my right ear becomes almost deafened. Sand and dirt rain down upon us while the green leaves trickle down more slowly to spread a layer of green over the crater.

While we rest in suspense for the barrage to cease, smoke and debris can be seen shooting above the undergrowth that stands in the center of the barrage. Shrapnel can be heard cutting the air strings as they squeal through the woods and air. The barrage takes its time about ceasing and so the lieutenant pulls us around the fire in order to continue the advance.

Before going much further, we are confronted with another cruel mess of machine-guns. All the Company have by now come to a halt. The officers detail squads to scout for machine-gun nests. This means that we hub——. The German machine works report from a forest beyond a wheat field. Good strategy. Surely in the event their enemy attempts to cross the field they will be lain to rest among the wheat. The enemy undoubtedly know we are in close vicinity judging from the growing reports of their guns. As the excitement grows more vociferous, cold chills run through my body. A shell adds to the horror when it bangs close by.

American soldiers are already attacking. Attacking from in front. The order to open fire is given. We fill the forest with bullets while men on the left rush from across the field. Bullets zip by by the hundreds. The men do not attempt to run all the way across the field at the same time. Part of them run while the rest lie crouched in the wheat. When those on foot lie down, those lying down jump and run. This is the way a machine-gun is attacked from the front.

Limbs and leaves fall among us. Bullets hiss above in swarms and some of them fall among us, kicking up dirt. A man being hit grabs a small bush squeezing it tightly with his hand, almost rolling over on his back and would if not for his pack. He throws his head back, grinds his teeth, slumps back on his belly, releases his hold on the bush and surrenders to death. It soon comes our turn to cross the field. We execute the command promptly but not by falling down too frequently in the wheat. The men are too anxious to make it to the woods to hesitate on the way across the field.

17. The Machine-Gun Engagements

The German gunners must be interrupted by our fire, as not nearly so many men as one would expect are being picked off. A great relief when I reach the woods. The men decline to run any further after reaching the woods. They lie down and begin shooting. They know the Germans are in the woods and hence, they are not to be dealt with kindly. Flying bullets strip the trees of their twigs and leaves. The Germans are not to be crushed so easily. Their guns still spray the ground and cut limbs from trees. A sergeant gasps nearby. Blood shoots from ear. He quivers; dying from a bullet in his brain. Small streaks of smoke are everywhere shooting from the top of the grass. I shoot up a clip of cartridges and feel for a bullet while I search my belt for another clip. The enemy fire seems to be coming from trees. They must be nested among the limbs. A gun to my right front is hushed. A vociferous rattle is heard. A heavy object bumps upon the ground. A nest is gone.

An hour later, the German machine-guns and Americans continue to quarrel at each other. But for the most part, each side has become far more quiet than at first. Americans lie wounded in the grass and among the underbrush. Some of them have already run the thermometers down. Some nurse their wounds with little or no criticism. Some nurse them while they bring down sworn exclamations upon some person they feel is responsible for them being wounded.

Empty cartridges lie over the ground. Some of them still smoke. The smoke stifles and we sneeze. Another gun cackles; bullets pour through and kick up dirt and cut grass blades. A sharp ring is heard upon my helmet. The helmet moves to one side. A dugout would be more than welcomed now. A breast-work should have been here all the time. We are caught in the snipers' path and here we lie at the mercy of Providence.

A medium-sized fellow, leaning backward supported by his pack, rubs his chest. He withdraws his hand from under his shirt and gestures as if to be feeling for someone's hand with which to comfort himself. The hand is smeared with his own blood. He strains for breath; he cannot get much air into his lungs. He moves his head from one side to the other. His eyes grow weaker. In a half whisper, he says, "Oh God! Why did it have to be?" He falls backward; dies. His face turns toward the ground. His pack holds him suspended; blood drips from his lips and coagulates upon the ground.

Men are trying to flank the gun. Again we are ordered to fire from the front. This concentrates the gunner's attention upon us. He again sends a covey of steel through the trees. They whistle above and among us. Leaves and twigs drop upon us. To hide behind a sapling no larger than a broom handle is some comfort. Men slide on their bellies to get in position to get a glance of the sniper. A flurry of bullets near them puts them on the ground from toe to eyeball. Officers can be heard saying, "Work in." I hear someone's mess-kit rattle. A bullet strikes it. The barrage centers in another direction; it is then that I have time to turn my head to one side to rest my neck. I see Red lying with his pack held in front of him. A splendid idea. Therefore, I remove my pack and lie it in front of myself and lie my rifle across it. When bullets come too close, I duck and hold the pack up so as to cover as much of my person as possible.

A rifle barrage reports to my left. The machine-gun ceases to fire. A suspense is lifted from my mind. I say, "Red, whose mess-kit was it that I heard rattle?"

"It must have been mine because I felt it rattle," he says.

The lieutenants give the platoons orders to work in close. Bushes shake. Men crawl forward, only to be met with a swarm of bullets again. Some of the wounded can be heard that cannot be seen. Most of them take to running to the rear on being wounded. They carry on babyishly and in some cases pitifully.

The Americans are fast flanking and surrounding the sniper. Should he happen to be stationed in a tree it will only be a question of time until he is dead or captured. If he is hidden on the ground and breasted with stones, he might be hard to get. In the event he does not intend to give up if he sees he is overpowered, it just means more deaths and casualties. The German has held the Americans back for some time. The enemy is doing his bit to hold us. He cannot hold out against so many of us all day.

The Americans blaze the forest with a fusillade of rifle bullets. They don't seem to do the work. The most thrilling event by our forces happens when a machine-gun is brought up behind us and opens fire in the direction of the German machine-gun. Leaves fall aplenty. The enemy machine is hushed for a few moments and opens again. The American gun swallows its clips like a cane mill does cane. Soon a stack of empty clips lie to the right of the machine-gun. The gun keeps up a loud fuss while the doughboys wedge to the left and right.

Bam! Something roars in the bushes. The machine is silenced. Bang! It happens again. It must all be over so far as the machine-gun is concerned. Everything is quiet. Even the American gun is resting. Men are heard talking loudly in front. Bushes can be heard moving. It all leads me to think the machine-gun nest is wiped out.

A few minutes later we are huddled around the German's dead body and his gun. His gun was stationed behind a large stack of stones with the muzzle protruding through a hole about the size of one's helmet. A grenaderian has put an end to all of it with a hand grenade. The man is the center of attraction for awhile and seems to get little kick out of telling just how he went about breaking up the nest. About all he says is that, "I saw him through the bushes and I let go of a grenade that luckily landed right."

Captain Woodside presents his tall figure through the underbrush. "Lieutenants, bring your men back here and help carry the wounded back into the edge of the swamp where they can be found by the Red Cross Force," he says.

I recognize most all the wounded but do not know all their names. I recognize some of the dead. Sergeant Vogt lies on his back dead. I count five bullet holes in his blouse. I relieve the dead body of what little corned beef and hard tack it has. Before I get through helping with the wounded, I have on my person four tins of beef and several hard tack.

A particular attraction is that of a wounded man fetched from among the bushes by four men who carry him supported on a blanket. The blanket is so saturated by blood that it drips almost in a stream upon the ground. He seems to be a favorite among those and one of them indicates it by saying, "Christ Almighty I hate this," then he unbuttons the dying man's blouse in order that he might be more comfortable. The blouse is saturated with blood and amidst all the blood one can see that he is plugged with several bullets. His blouse and shirt having been unbuttoned reveals that he received a cluster of bullets under the right teat. His skin spotted with several holes smaller than the end of one's little finger, blood oozes out the openings when he tries to breathe. While waiting in suspense for the victim to force another breath of air, he fails to respond by having taken the path into eternity.

Seeing that their friend is dead, one of the men writes a note and sticks it in a buttonhole of the dead man's blouse. The contents of the note are, "Please see that no part of this man's body is visible when you bury him." The men fix the blanket over the corpse so as to hide his entire body and leave to carry heavy crosses until they meet the same fate or until they reach a hospital. I say "hospital" in compliment to Good Fortune, for it seems that if any of us get through that luckily, we ought to fold our hands in reverence to God.

A group of about twenty slightly injured men stand and sit huddled under a beech tree. Some of them are wounded in the hand; some in the leg; some carry scratches about their faces and some have slight wounds about the body. Some of them laugh and carry on while some of them try to make it appear that they are the worst wounded fellow on the front to yet be on foot. A fellow whose name is Miller makes the grouchiest of them smile when he cracks the following joke: "I have a son back in Richmond, Virginia and if the Son of a ***** ever steps off on his left foot I'll kill him." Of course you will agree this is a cruel joke but if you could just understand how meaningless this joke was and how well it broke the monotony up here on Hell's Point, you would smile yourself.

Lucky is he that comes through whole and only carrying slight wounds. Luckier, it seems, is he that receives slight wounds; for such a wound means, only, a rest and temporary relief from the many means of hungry death that at all times hangs over everyone up here on this cruel front. Even the trees are sore from wounds and still stand exposed to the resistance of both enemies while they shoot and bombard each other trying to settle a dispute that each and every man is innocent of.

Right now more machine-guns can be heard fussing back in the forest. The men that operate them do not know why they shoot each other than that they shoot just because they are told to. And the fact that some of them are locked and chained to their guns is definite assurance that they do not know why they are supposed to shoot. Summing it all up, it every bit seems just like a pack of foolishness. It seems that a lot of jealousy, envy and domineering pride bosomed by those who have not yet heard a shell burst are being resented at the sacrifice of the innocent, ordinary, poor and laboring class of people.

18

My Personal Machine Encounter

The Company assembles under some trees close to the crying wounded; some of those wounded are feeling the effect more now as their wounds grow sorer. It is easy to tell that the Company loses several men through either being wounded or killed. Three sergeants and two lieutenants are missing, beside a lot of privates and corporals. I gaze out into space and wonder why it is that I have not got picked off yet. Guess my time will be next, I think, or maybe not at all here. Who can tell?

The officers decide that since it means such a great loss to attack the nests in such large groups, it might be best to attack with smaller units. Hence, we are sent out into the deathly forest in squads to locate and if possible to destroy the machine-gun nests. Each squad is given a certain direction to pursue. The officer that directs my squad says, "You must locate something before you return. If you don't think you can do the job with the squad alone, return and summon support."

These are orders; official orders. We must obey, knowing we are to soon walk into the mouth of hungry hell and be chewed up. The lieutenant says to me, "Since your corporal has been wounded, I appoint you to take charge of the squad and bring back a German machine-gunner."

I salute and say, "Very well, lieutenant. We shall do our best."

We are off. The distance between each unit grows greater as we penetrate the forest. The men move reluctantly. They possess an attitude that prompts them not to go. They look at one another with questionable countenances. Red says, "Hell! Those damned officers ought to be right here with us telling us how to go about it all."

In my own heart, I quietly agree with him but keep silent. I know Lieutenant Singletary is as brave as anyone and it is not through cowardice that he is not here trying to spot them with us. He is honest in what he is directing.

The men drag their feet more and more reluctantly through the grass as they trudge along. We have not gone a hundred yards yet. The machine-guns can be heard with more audibility as we move into the trees. The report becomes more of a cackle than of a clack the further we get. Our hearts flutter and kick enough to almost cause our blouses to vibrate. We know death confronts us not any piece up there. It seems that death barks from every limb. The trees themselves, seem to grow resentful and unaccommodating. It seems that there is not a friend this side of the Atlantic. The officers have no mercy for us. They drive us straight into the doors of death. Are we afraid? Are we not? Take your choice.

The men become too weak-hearted. They tell me that they do not intend to go any further. I say, "I dread it as much as you. I do not crave going on and risking my only life trying to get them but you know it is orders and we must do something to show that we made an attempt. Let's try. Maybe we will get through all right."

One of them says, "It is a pack of damned foolishness to go up here and try to take a machine-gun nest when they are hidden away in trees ready to mow us down when we approach."

I urge them to come along a little further and that if we cannot find any nests we will return to the Company and report none. I lead on thinking they might follow. They refuse to follow and finally pull themselves in the direction of an opening of a wheat field. I loudly urge them repeatedly to come on up. They refuse emphatically and becoming disgusted with trying to coax them on, I take it on myself to penetrate the forest a little further just to satisfy myself that I had carried out, to some extent, orders.

A few minutes later, I find myself standing by the root of a beech tree not realizing that I stood a victim before an unmerciful machine-gun that roosted in a nearby tree to mow me down like a stalk of grass or wheat. I should not have guessed that a machine-gun rested perched on the limbs of a tree so close by. The chatter of a gun not more than fifty yards, it seems, cuts through the leaves and brush nearby. Bullets zip and hiss by my head. Bark flies from the trunk of the tree and flips against my face, leading me to believe that it is bullets cutting my facial exposure. My faculties being so mesmerized, I have to think twice before I know that my position should not be perpendicular but horizontal instead. Hence, I flop down upon my belly and lie hovered by the tall grass to wait for a bullet or more to plug me through-and-through sending me into the land among the stars. It is only when one is expecting every breath to be the last one that he can imagine so many events that have taken place through life and imagine every one of them to have been good. Even the worst I ever had, I can now believe I should have relished!

The gun incessantly fires upon me. I feel that I wish a bullet would end it all since I know it is impossible to stand alive here again. The suspense is enough to kill one to say nothing of a bullet that it seems will be sure to draw a curtain over it all in a few moments. I can feel bark falling upon my neck and helmet. I can hear bullets kicking up dirt close to me. Were it possible to drop in a hole, I would give twenty years of my life. Destiny has me hand-cuffed; that is all and I just know I will here rot. I can imagine some soldiers chunking me in a shell hole, flipping a little dirt over me and leaving me to fill the air with my rotten stink until nothing remains but my white frame.

Why does not one end it! Why does not one end it! There are the questionable thoughts that pass through my mind as I lie as sure prey to the heartless steel demon that keeps vigil over me until it is certain that I am as full of holes as a window screen. I squeeze my eyelids so tight as to almost drive my eyeballs to the back of my head. It is suspense that prompts me to abuse every muscle in my body in response to the deadly threats of that barking hell up there among the limbs of a tree. A greedy dog could not keep any closer vigil over a piece of meat as the gun keeps over me. It rattles; it won't stop; I lie as still as possible thinking I might lead the gunner to believe I am dead. Maybe they all don't fall close to me but it seems that they do.

The gun ceases to fire. The heavy suspense momentarily lifts and it seems that a thousand-pound object could not have made things seem lighter. Should I be able to conceal myself behind the tree, I might be safe. This is the one thought that my mind will not give up. I become more and more prompted to execute this idea. I cannot make up my mind to lie here exposed to the machine-gun for if the operator should even see me breathe, it would all be to do over. I adjust all my muscles preparatory to coming to my all fours and bouncing behind the tree. Coming to my feet the gun is heard opening up again. Perhaps it is just a plain coincidence and not meant for me. However, nothing can make me believe it is not. I can feel the weight of the mown grass as I come to my feet. Fearing that the attempt reaching a position behind the tree will end fatally, I fall once again to be terribly picked on by the enemy in the tree. I again feel for a bullet to end it all. Were I back in safety, I feel that I could kick myself for using such poor strategy in trying to find safety when maybe I was already safe as a result of the gunner probably thinking I was dead. It all amounts to the fact that I am too anxious to get out, plain force of the bullets. The gun again ceasing fire, I make up my mind to take position behind the tree even if I had to do it while the gun was operating at me. Jumping up, a machine-gun greatly excites me by vociferously rattling a little to my right. I do not look around to see anything. I just know it is another German gun and that my time is at hand. The excitement causing me to act involuntarily, I run into an old treetop and soon find myself fastened in a mass of strong seasoned limbs. My rifle strap gets fastened; my hobnails are clumsy among the limbs; I just cannot make any headway; everything is against my getting away without being killed. This is my time, and all the efforts I might put into use to evade it are all in vain. I am being tantalized good before the fatal bullet puts my lights out.

These thoughts flash through my mind by the time it takes a bullet to zip by. A passion of anger flashes through me. I turn around and look; I hear something making a fuss. Something rattles; something shakes the limbs of a tree as though a bear were playing upon them; I can see them move briskly as they shake in response to some heavy object misbehaving on them. Something rattles; something large and bulky bumps the limbs jarring them heavily in the descent to the ground; I can see the object falling. It bumps with a loud thud upon the ground; the rattling object follows it crashing upon the ground a second later. I quickly twist my neck as I anxiously look back over my shoulder in the direction of the last machine-gun I heard. Three Americans stand behind the covering of a large shell hole. One of them says, "We got him." The operator of the gun drags the gun from the top of the dugout. He smiles but is reticent. The others jabber between each other with fancy. My intense scare sort of leaving me, I yell out, "Yes and you just about scared me to death."

"What are you doing there?" one of them asks.

"I am here because I am forced to it," I reply.

I learn through the men that they slipped up behind the dugout and killed the German machine-gunner while his attention was drawn upon me.

It is by another miracle, it seems, that I was once again spared from what seemed to be certain death. I feel more than happy to have come through alive again. The men all smoke and I smoke with them; my first cigarette in years but the excitement and then joy of it all brings to my senses the old instinctive desire to smoke. I soon find myself reporting back to the Company my experiences to find the other men safe and unexcited sprawled out upon the ground ready to ask me what all I saw. One of them says, "I thought sure you got killed." "Why" he says, "we were right on that gun ourselves when it opened up."

"And when it opened up you ran as hard as you could, didn't you?" I ask him.

Opening a tin of corned beef, Sergeant Easterly and I munch upon it while we recall the happenings of the day and tell of this one and that one that got killed or wounded. He listens interestingly with a mouth full of beef that gives him the appearance of having a swollen jaw from toothache as I give an account of my recent experiences. He chuckles deeply and then follows with, "It's Hell!"

19

Passing the Night

It is by now, about four o'clock in the afternoon. Everything on the front is at unrest yet. Bullets still zip around cutting twigs and leaves from trees. We have fought among trees all day; have been handicapped by having to advance through underbrush. The enemy have had the "ups" on us as the expression goes. They have taken the advantage of us through squatting behind their mowing machines and putting it into operation when they were sure they would be able to stack us up on one another. But one side or the other had to advance. So it were we that did it; it were we that suffered so many losses either by receiving wounds or by being claimed by death.

I cannot tell you one fiftieth of what has gone up here today. Should I be able to, you would marvel at it all. I am able, only, to tell you of just a little of what happened right in my immediate vicinity. The excitement has been so intense all the way through that I could not concentrate for any length of time on anything.

There has been practically no shelling during the last few hours. The men on both sides have been in too close quarters for either side to try and shell its enemy. It might have resulted in either battery killing its own men. It has been a fight for the greater part between the American infantry and German machine-guns all day since crossing the Marne. The Americans have been successful with respect to taking territory but on the other hand have suffered a one-sided loss compared with the Germans. The forest has been spotted with machine-gun nests and used extensively against us all day. The German infantry have not functioned against us today. Perhaps it will give us a reception tomorrow.

The sun is concealing itself beyond the trees. Soon it will be hidden and darkness will pull a curtain over us and shield us while either enemy matches wits through planning to kill each other tomorrow. The men sent out to scout for machine-gun nests have about all returned. Practically all of them report having not seen or spotted any nests.

The Company commander informs us that we will scour the woods as far as a wheat field beyond the forest. There, he says, we will occupy a position for the night.

We rest quietly in the edge of the woods adjoining the field. Darkness is fast pulling a shade over the faces of the men. Machine-guns can be heard barking out there among the wheat. Bullets zip over and around us as much as to say, "You will have no rest tonight."

The grass stinks with the odor of high explosives and gases. It all adds to the aggravation the machine-guns out there deal out to us. I just cannot close my eyes. I am too nervous. A bullet might catch me napping; a German might walk up and plug me while I snore away. The remembrances and shocks I received all day rest upon and worry my mind. I can see the men falling in the river; I can see the man as his fingers gradually relax upon the bridge, giving his body up to the belly of the Marne's cold waters. I can see the blubbers trickling upward to the surface as the victim is being gulped into the bottom of the river. I can hear the men out there in the underbrush and forest struggling for that which is most essential to life: Air. I can see the man in the bushes as he closes his fingers on the trunk of the sapling to a few seconds later relax them in response to the call of death. I can see the man as he looks into my eyes asking for a match with which to light a cigarette to quiet his nerves and pacify his stirred mind. I can hear the mortally wounded soldier begging for someone to drag him from the center of the barrage in order that he can die just a little like a man should die. I can see the blood dripping from the blanket as the mortally wounded man's buddies fetch him out of the brush to find later that he had caught a handful of bullets in his left side. I can see the crimson blubber oozing from the man's side. I can see his eyes setting upon his place among the stars. All these sad and cruel events are visible upon my mind. I try to drive them out of my presence but cannot. My eyes feel weak and burning. To close them might mean fatality. My mental state won't allow me to close them. My mind is mad with possession of the many visions of the day. I find my eyes trying to pierce the darkness when a shell howls over or when a bullet hisses through the limbs. My nerves dominate my whole body and I just cannot control them.

A man or two stir in the rear. I hear my name called. I respond. I am advised that I will sit as sentry during part of the night.

"You will take your position now and keep watch until midnight," the detail man says.

He carries me to my post. A small pile of short posts lie near my position. I take up watch behind them as they will be of use as breast-work against bullets. So far as I know no one is within a hundred yards of me now. There is nothing for companionship save the cackle of the machine-guns more distant in front. I feel more lonely than ever before in my life. Even the breezes that fan the leaves seem to taunt and hate me. I am, myself, mad at everything.

A starr-shell rises in the distance on the enemy side. I can see it as it hangs suspended in the air. It is through the limbs of the trees that I see it as it moves slowly, its rays piercing the forest. The shadows of everything move with it. They move as if completing a circle. The shell gradually burns out leaving everything again hovered under complete darkness. Signal rockets decorate the sky on the enemy side. They are beautiful to watch. Should this be a friendly display, it would be a remarkable picture for a wooing couple to watch and enjoy as each filled the other's heart with words of love and compliments.

An hour or more later, the report of arms of any sort cannot be heard. Everything seems to be enjoying the wee hours of the night. The enemies seem to have shaken hands and agreed to call it a peaceful night. But my mind still bears the mad visions of the day and will not allow me to raise the white flag.

Midnight still finds me in an alarming condition. My nerves are yet but little settled. It still boils with the horrible remembrances of the day. I can imagine I hear things when I very much doubt that I do. It seems that I can hear gases making fusses in dead bodies. I think I hear wounded men mumbling out there in the bushes. I think I hear persons walking with loud steps. I imagine I am being surrounded by German patrolmen. It is under the suffering of these visions and imaginations that I lie here miserable when the late hours of midnight announce their approach.

Again I think I hear the trampling of feet and the shaking of bushes. They come nearer and nearer. My heart thumps loudly. I can hear my own blood swishing through my head. I bring my rifle to my shoulder. It almost jumps from my feeble clutches. I think I hear words of my own language spoken. It seems that they come from among the bushes in the direction of the moving objects. I just cannot squeeze the trigger. I cannot even find it. "Hey sentry," someone says.

"On post," I answer.

"This man will relieve you," the corporal of the guard says.

It is now that I recollect that I was to be relieved at midnight. Returning to my place in my squad, I sprawl out upon the ground to nurse nervous chills until the breaking of day brings with it a swarm of bullets that zip and hiss over us as a remembrance from the Germans out there in the wheat.

20

Almost Surrounded

Daylight drives darkness away. The Germans seem to be hostile to the former's coming. The enemy's bullets again breathe through to pass through the leaves and twigs or bury themselves in the limbs and trunks of trees. They can be heard spatting against trees. Men begin to straighten out their legs and drive the humps from their spines preparatory to taking as safe positions as possible upon their bellies. The early morning does not bring to our ears the mooing of cows, the whinnying of horses, the crow of the cock, the bleat of the ewe, the report of mother's feet in the kitchen as she prepares breakfast, the sound of trains as they move in the distance. No, indeed, the good old comforting sounds back there do not ring in our ears here. While they are not heard up here, it is here that we really and wholeheartedly appreciate them. No! They are not heard up here in this forest where men try madly to take one another's lives for an unknown cause. Maybe for no cause at all. Men who have never seen or heard of one another hold deathly grievances and would like to smack out each others' lives.

The hungry call prompts several of us to open tins of beef under a shower of bullets. It is when I smell some of it that is being eaten near me that I reach in my overcoat pocket and bring a tin of it in front of me, open it, and scrunch upon it and hard tack. Our bellies are empty and we relish our meal. It is now that I again recall the old recollections of my friend, Ben Jarrel; it is now that I more than any time appreciate his big heart; it is now I am sure he would be glad to give me another big, hot, juicy feed.

Here it is that we hear the hum of the enemies' planes, the report of the enemies' cannons, the cackle of the enemies' machine-guns. If all this up here should turn out to be a dream, I am sure all those on awaking would jump and hug the trees in response to joy. But the reports of the enemy arms means that our blood is wanted. We will continue to feed them today, tomorrow, in the future.

The wheat cut there shakes as the bullets fly through it. A fellow not ten feet from me already lies dead with one of the sniping steel balls lodged in his body. Another carries a wounded foot as result of the early morning's hostilities. Twigs and leaves fall upon us the same as yesterday. We again face the same manner of death that claimed so many of our men yesterday. What will be the outcome by night?

A machine-gun rattles across the corner of the field in the woods beyond. The report is followed by a flurry of bullets that whistle over and among us. Dirt is kicked up among us, and a man has already received one of the presents in his pack. It goes through the blanket but does not harm the man. Another swarm of bullets find me and my pack behind a small tree. Not another tree stands between me and the opening of the field. I see the wheat shake as the bullets beat through it. I can hear small arms banging in the field and across the field in the swamp. I can hear shells banging in the rear. I can hear them as they swish through the air to fall a tenth of a second later in the swamp back of us. It seems that the enemy is more determined than ever to stop us. The machine-guns rattle and fuss as much as to say, "You shall not pass." It all cannot be machine-gun fire. It all sounds like a mixture of machine-guns and rifle fire. Gosh! I guess the infantry is moving against us or else wait entrenched to mow us down if we try to pass. A machine-gun swings its range upon my tree and bullets beat madly against it. I crouch like a squirrel hiding upon a limb. Bombs fall closer than ever today. They burst nearby sending straw, grass, and dirt spurting into the air. The animals of the field and forest are excited and on the run. Birds can be seen flying by with the speed of a shell. The scared fowls seem to know that everything has turned out to be their enemy. They fly in haste trying to seek safety somewhere. Rabbits are scared as I am and run here and thither trying to move out of the extreme danger that they must surely think is all meant for them. I can hear a bomb roaring through the air. Judging from the approach it intends lighting close by. By the time it lights, a rabbit bounces in front of me and I swear I am blown to pieces. It is fully a minute before I am convinced that my head has not been blown from my shoulders. My heart flutters loudly and should I have heart trouble later I know this experience will be the reason.

I can hear a machine just across the corner of the field. The report indicates that it is nearby. I peek around the tree to look for the gun. It rattles. I can see the leaves fan and move as the gun sends its concussion among them. I discover a red object upon the limb. I withdraw my hand and conceal it behind the tree when a swarm of bullets hiss above and over us. A man nearby grabs his side and runs to the rear seemingly greatly excited. He utters, "Oh, me" as he seeks the rear. Several men now lie wounded or dead from the barrage of bullets. A man in my rear lies snatching grass from the ground and writhing in pain from the effects of a bullet that has lodged in his body. He slings his helmet to one side as if he blames it for the unfortunate happening. He lies with his head exposed to the barrage. The gun in the tree changing its range, I again look around the tree to try and locate the gunner. I again see the red object among the leaves. Aha! I have him spotted. He will bump the ground as soon as I get my rifle to my shoulder. He does not know that I have my eye on him. He is not aware that I will have my rifle on him within a second's time. He probably has not dreamed since nesting in that tree that an American will lie him upon the ground to rot. If he hasn't ever dreamed, he has missed his chance. I hug my rifle stock tightly. The bullet is certain to pierce the red object; then the German's head. He will bump the ground. I hate tree–Germans; one of them scared the wits out of me yesterday and besides did his best to kill me. Now is my time for revenge. The expression, "turn about is fair play," holds true here. I turn my head a little to one side while I practice my victory smile. It is all just too good not to get a little kick out of it before it is all over. My heart beats loudly at the thought of the welcomed thrill. His old gun will be hushed now. I am about doing a great deed for my country and my fellow men. I am avenging those he has killed and wounded. I must set quickly or someone will beat me to it. These are the thoughts that entertain my mind while I am bringing my rifle to my shoulder to drop him. Bang! I reload while I expect to be entertained by watching the Heinie spill upon the ground. My mind clicks with surprise. I must be too nervous to shoot, I think. I sight down my rifle barrel. It quivers some but not so much as to keep me from dropping that sniper. Bang! The German remains stationary. My confidence and thrill begin to fade a little. Bang! Bang! Bang! I empty my rifle at the red object. The machine-gun ceases firing but no German falls from the tree. I nurse surprise. I reload. Again I bang at the object and what I take to be the treeman's head five times more. The object still remains unstirred. A knot comes in my throat. I am no good. I should be back some place where someone is needed that cannot shoot straight. "Why can't I kill the guy?" is my thought. I recalled that I qualified the second time I shot on the rifle range in camp. I feel something punch me in my side. I look around to find that a heavily built, ugly rough-looking fellow had crawled up by my side to find out what all the trouble is about. He says, "What is it you are shooting at so much?"

"I see the red band on a German's cap in that tree, but I cannot kill the German," I reply.

"What tree is it?" he asks. I point to the tree. He gazes through his fiery eyes a few seconds, brings his rifle to his shoulder, and sights. He moves his face to be sure that his heavy, rough jaw fits snugly against the rifle stock. Confidence is written all over him. Bang! Smoke comes from the bore of his rifle. I keep close vigil on the tree. Limbs shake; leaves tremble noisily; the tree acts as if it intends to take feet and walk off. Something rattles. I can see a small object drop from the lower limbs; something bumps the limbs heavily; a large grey object appears fast falling to the ground; it bumps the ground with a loud thud; the gun rattles but does not complete the fall. The German lies under the tree dying or dead. The man by me doesn't seem any more excited than if he were resting somewhere in seclusion.

"You son of a gun," I say to him. "I wanted him."

"You see the cap is still there, don't you?" he asks.

"I see it is," I answer.

"If you shoot the cap and he don't fall, look somewhere else and you will find him."

He discharges a handful of tobacco juice heavily upon the ground and says, "If that won't work, take a big chew of tobacco and you can even see the white of his eyes."

He chuckles and crawls away.

20. Almost Surrounded

Bark flies from my protecting tree. I keep close. There is no need shooting until I can see something to shoot at. My nerves are again seeking an aggravating tension. It took them all night to quiet down just a little bit. I lived through it yesterday; perhaps darkness again will find me alive. It is all too uncertain to hold much hope.

A man is on his feet walking through the bushes as if he means to walk right out into the field and give himself for a German target. He has a Chau-Chaut rifle hanging by his side. He pulls his helmet down over his eyes and face. He must be mad. He enters the opening of the field and starts shooting his gun. "You are crazy," I yell. "Get down before you are killed." He is nearby me but pays no heed. He continues shooting until his clip of bullets has been exhausted. He walks further out into the wheat. He removes the empty clip and replaces it with a loaded one. He opens again and shoots several times. I hear machine-gun cackle; the man crouches, groans, slumps forward and falls upon his face. He folds himself almost double and signals intense pain with deathly groans. The wheat almost hides the dying body. A few minutes later the dead body begins to chill. The horror of it all must have had a mad effect on the slain man for ordinarily Sergeant Easterday would have not even thought of pulling such a dastardly and foolish prank.

The sergeant's hopes have gone out into space. He will never see his sister educated. Probably as he lay in the grass here, he thought of the insurance his folks would get should he be slain in France. Probably he figured it would mean more to them than he. Perhaps his love for his mother and sister was more than his love for his own life. Perhaps that is the real cause of his walking out and giving his life to the enemy, who relished it.

At the end of another period of suspense, the enemy seems as much determined as ever that we will not advance. The machine-guns bark as vociferously as ever. Something tells me the enemy's strength is being increased. I can hear it; I can feel it.

German planes are now fanning the tops of the trees, hovering low down. They roar loudly as they start over the trees and field. Their actions seem to indicate that they mean to light in the field. They have not thought of such a thing, however. They circle over the trees as though they are anxious to know our exact position. They bombard the swamp to our rear; the report comes towards us. They know we are in the woods but they do not know exactly where.

The underbrush moves in the rear. Someone tells to retreat quietly. He says, "Move back quietly. Do not let them know we are on the retreat."

"What does it all mean?" I ask myself. The officers must figure our opposition is too great, and hence, mean to pull us out of range of their guns. We crawl and move back slowly. Someone comes near me.

"What does all this mean?" I ask. He shakes his head indicating he does not know.

Lieutenant Singletary appears before us. He says, "Follow me and make it snappy." By this time we are out of danger of any Germans seeing us. The officer moves with quick steps through the woods. I know we are in danger but I cannot surmise as to the nature of it. I move up behind the lieutenant and say, "Why do we retreat, Lieutenant?"

He looks back over his shoulder and says, "We are almost surrounded."

I discover that we are being pulled quietly out of almost certain captivity. We are almost imprisoned within a circle of heartless Germans. I feel relieved, too, to no longer be such closer prey for the enemies' machine-guns. Some of the men seem not to be able to move fast enough. The lieutenant stops abruptly, turns around, and says, "We must move down close to the river. Most of the Company is ahead of us. If they cut us off at the river, we are as good as gone." He points to a field to our right, gapes with surprise and says, "Look!" Through the openings of the trees and bushes, the helmets and backs of the Germans can be seen as the enemy moves down through the field to cut us off at the river.

"Pull to the left," the lieutenant says. A few seconds later we are out of the enemy's view and moving fast down toward the river.

A machine-gun is heard to our right front. It cannot be an enemy machine-gun. It must be trying to play a role in stopping the advancing enemy. It makes me feel good to hear it. Anything to give the Heinies competition would be welcomed. I wonder why the officer did not give us orders to fire upon the visible Germans. I conclude finally that his motive in such action is to lead them to think we do not know their intentions.

20. Almost Surrounded

A few minutes later we are some distance from the enemy. No doubt they still believe we are further up in the forest. The river can be seen from where we are. But we shall not continue any further in that direction. There are not enough trees to conceal us. The Company commander's orders are that we must cross a wheat field that separates the forest as the quickest retreat out of danger of being captured. He seems to be wise enough to know that a few hundred men cannot whip as many Germans as seem to be opposing us.

The Company assembles near the opening of the field. The officers distribute the men at various points alongside the field where they are sent across in single file. Luckily, I do not have to cross first expecting my head to be shot off any time while crossing. I expect every second for the first men crossing to be shot down. They make it across and no one can measure their joy. As my time to cross gets nearer, I can hear rifles popping above us in the field or in the edge of the swamp just across the field. Now I wish I could have crossed first of all.

The Germans are nearing us all the time. We must cross, fight or give up. Their firearms pop closer. Just what manner of strategy they use in pursuing us so closely is unknown. My time comes to cross over. Red crosses with me. I fear that we are in a circle of enemies. I load; he follows. The captain and a few of the men remain behind. I try to shield all my person below the top of the wheat as I run along. Firearms bang nearby; bullets hiss by and strike the wheat. Before I realize it, I am flat upon my belly working my way down a small incline sparsely covered with wheat. I work backwards on my belly. Through haste and excitement, I forget all about Red and only remember that he was to cross over with me when I hear him breathing loudly as he, too, works to his rear upon his belly.

I lie my face flat on the ground. I keep working myself back so as to seek a safe place to conceal my body. I become exhausted and stop for a short rest. Red stays close by me. He puffs with exhaustion. His face is as red as a cock's comb. Sweat pours from his brow. He is excited and realizes that we are again facing the deathly sting of the enemy. We both pant like an ox in the hot sun. I discover that I dropped my raincoat in my fall to the ground and that it lies about seven or eight feet in front of me. Red has also dropped his raincoat. He says he intends

111

to try and get it. I say, "Red, get mine too while you are getting yours." Red comes to his all fours to be received with a swarm of bullets that swish close to him. The intensity of the excitement arouses his anger and flopping quickly upon his belly, he screams, "Get your own damned raincoat."

My lips quiver a little in response to the little bit of comedy he furnishes. The fire ceasing, Red again attempts to get his coat. Being naturally very tall he is handicapped in concealing himself below the top of the wheat. He almost reaches his coat; bullets follow the reports of rifles. Red nearly turns a backwards somersault as he falls back down the incline. He rolls against me. I cannot conceive that his actions are due to fright and

response to seek safety this time. They are too inactive and misdirected. He must be hit. "Are you hit, Red?" I ask. He quivers. "What is the matter, Red?" I ask again. He fails to answer. I know he is dying now. I slide to one side and dying Red rolls partly upon his back. His pack holds him partly upon his side and back. He struggles. His eyes almost turn over in their sockets. He strains for breath and what little air that is carried into his lungs with his unconscious, remaining strength causes a gurgling with the blood in his neck. I think of giving him water but remember that my canteen has been empty several hours. I feel for his canteen and it, too, is as empty as my own. He seems to try to reach a good deep breath but cannot. He struggles a few more times and then lies dead. His lips turn white; the color leaves his face. It all means he was meant to rot here in this field. A lump comes in my throat. I cannot help but grieve at the loss of Red. He was a good sort and meant no harm in anything he did or said. He has fought bravely all the way through. He has never once thought of crumbling under his duty as a lineman. He could always be seen in the front firing with the rest of the men. I liked him; he seemed to like me.

A few minutes after Red fell, the captain walks out into the opening in the wheat. A few men follow him. He talks loudly as if angry about something. Nearing me, I yell at him to lie down. He says, "What are you fellows lying there for? Why don't you beat it across the field?"

He only becomes convinced that he stands there ready to be shot down when I inform him that the man by my side is dead. He looks anxiously at Red's body and then yells, "Let's all get out of here quickly."

I cannot make up my mind to be left behind to bear the fate of the enemy. Hence, I gain my feet and run with the rest of them, expecting every step to be brought down. No one but I can realize the extent of my relief on reaching the woods.

21

Turning the Tide

More than an hour later finds the Company out of temporary captivity. We are crouched in crudely constructed trenches in an opening overlooking the Marne. We have eluded captivity by one enemy; but did it at the expense of a few men. It is discouraging and hurtful to have part of the ground that we paid so dearly for retaken by the stubborn Germans.

They might now be trampling over the bodies of the dead; they might now be examining Red's and Easterday's body for ration and souvenirs. The dead have given their blood to mingle with the sods of this Champaigne Marne forest for a cause some of them believed to be right and for a cause some of them believed not to be right.

The ground is seeded with machine-gun bullets and pitted and pimpled with high explosives this and the other side of the river, the result of the invincible trying to check us. Up until this morning we have been heroically successful in gaining territory but at the cost of many men who were either wounded or killed. The machine-guns and hell fire have dealt out plenty of misery for us. Many an American now lies rotting upon or under the sods of the Marne from their effects. Many Americans lie nursing their wounds from their stings. Those who still live are furrow-faced and nearly exhausted from fatigue and diarrhea. Our eyes are sunken and red; our faces are beardy and trenched, causing us to look fifteen years older. Never prior to the night of the 14th did we appreciate civil life and the friendship of our neighbors and our dogs. We appreciate them now; our bosoms are bulged with appreciations.

The suns beams down upon us in this shallow, rocky trench. Its rays seem to mesmerize us through sympathy with our enemy. We sit here in the hot, boiling sun nearly dying under the heat while our determined enemy occupies the shaded ground we suffered to conquer; the ground that my nerves failed upon. My canteen is as dry as the top of a cook stove; my throat is parching for a swig of water; my tongue feels like a sponge in my dry mouth. The taste of beef is still in my mouth and that too makes me feel like I could drink the Marne River dry.

The German machine-guns bark more boastful than any time previously. Rifles crack not so very far up there in the woods. They might be moving down upon us. Let them come; we are entrenched, and they won't be if they come. We will have the advantage of them. They come. They can be seen moving around the corner of an opening. We fire upon them. They scatter and return the fire. The bullets whistle over our heads and beat upon the parapet. The parapet is not much protection; therefore, we have to protect ourselves as much as possible below the surface of the trench. My rifle seems to operate slowly. It just won't work as fast as I want it to. It must be because the Germans are so close upon us. The Americans seem to be well organized judging from the amount of the fire they deliver. Our cannons even seem to know what it is all about. They shell the swamp where the enemy is advancing, madly. The advancing Germans kneel before our fire. That does not check them; they still come. Shells swish over our heads and a tenth of a second later light among the Germans blowing them into atoms. A man to my right receives a wound in his arm. He carried a Chau-Chau rifle. He can use it no more. So I grab it and let it bark at them. I sling two bags of clips to the man on my left and tell him to find my gun while I work on them. I sling one over my shoulder and then finish the clip the wounded man left unused. I turn it loose on a wave of the enemy I see moving around a patch of bushes. Some of them fall; some of them run. A group of Germans appear from the bushes to my left. I quickly focus my rifle in that direction but then find that the Heinies hold their hands above their heads. They seem greatly alarmed, and act quickly when they are told or motioned to pass on to the rear; they quickly obey.

Through my own excitement, I find myself trying to operate an empty gun. I storm at the man to watch his business and keep my gun loaded. He lies humped in the bottom of the trench trembling from head to foot. "What is the matter with you?" I yell.

"I think I'm shell shocked," he replies.

"Yes, that's what they all say when they are scared to death," I scream.

I realize more fully than ever that we must act more quickly and more sanely than ever since being on the front lest we are massacred right here. Grabbing my faculties together, I adjust a clip and open up in the direction they have been coming. True, I do not see any Germans advancing but I know they are subject to doing it and hence I intend to beat them at their own game. My gun rattles. It is almost drowned by other guns in the trench. I clamp my teeth as I shoot. I do not feel that we can allow them to pass or take any more of the ground we have conquered. I feel more like fighting than any time since I have been up here. I really would like to kill some of them. I carry almost as heavy grievance for the man humped in the trench as I do for the Germans. He should help us stop them. He still trembles and when the fire lightens, looks up and says, "Do you see any now?"

"Why don't you get up and see for yourself?" I growl. Seeing five Germans running in our direction giving themselves up, I yell, "There they come again." He crouches again. I laugh and then look down upon his crouching figure and say, "You cowardly hound."

The prisoners smile as they jump the trench as much as to say, "We are glad we are your prisoners."

These are the last Germans we see for the day. My fright seems to have left me and I honestly feel that I could endure another attack from the grey uniforms. My nerves seem to be more steady than any time during the past few days. While bringing my rifle inside the trench, I catch hold of the barrel and hastily release it because it is too hot. Adjusting my pack under my head, I lie down in the shallow trench and laugh until my sides hurt; not because there is anything funny to laugh about, but because I am so glad we turned the tide.

We lie huddled in the trench for a good while. The sun is hotter than ever. Sweat rolls down our faces, and it seems that we will melt under the hot rays. The rocks seem to give off as much heat as the sun itself. The wounded man to my right holds his arm. His hand is bloody from holding the wound. He crawls from the trench, sprawls out upon the ground and says, "I can't help it if they kill me; I just can't stay in that trench and burn up." He lies outside the trench for some time and seeing that nothing detrimental from the enemy befalls him, most all the rest of us follow suit.

We are burning up inside from thirst. Our mouths are as dry as the Sahara. We must have water if we have to go all the way to the Marne for it, risking ourselves to be killed. Someone suggests that we hunt water. I accept the challenge and soon four of us are out to satisfy our thirst. We hunt a path or some indication of the direction of the river. We fail to find the path, but as Providence directs it, we come across a crude makeshift of stony steps that lead up and down a steep hill. Ascending the steps but not dreaming we would run into water, we stop abruptly when we hear the sound of water pouring upon something. Hastening to the report of the falling object, we find a fountain of flowing water in the rear of a small stone structure constructed in the side of the hill. Being the first to reach the structure, I slide inside and fill the other fellows' canteens and tell them that is the last they will get before I fill my belly all the way to my tonsils. Wrapping my mouth around the spout, I fill up well and good, then reach back for the others' canteens that have long since become empty. Feeling so happy from the effects of the cold water that has gone so far in making us feel relieved and from having whipped the Germans and having put them on the run again, we sit down, smoke, and talk loudly of it all. Hardly any of our experiences coincide.

We return to the trench, report the finding of the water, and lie around all day thinking mostly of the good things back in the U.S.A. The coming of darkness finds us getting ready to move out of the forest where we have fought strenuously to make our objective a record and where we have suffered unbelievable hardships and almost unbearable nervous strains.

Whether anyone else will ever agree that we carried our duty to expectations or not, we move out of the Champaigne Forest to never again shoot at or be shot at by the Germans.

22

Return to Crezancy

Night comes on and we travel in the direction of the Marne. What a relief to know we are moving in opposite direction to the German lines. The elements and earth nearly are lighted with the ascend-flares on the enemy's side and add to our relief, the flares seeming to be further back than last night.

We cross the Marne with far more satisfaction than before. It is evident now that we are returning to Crezancy. The dead still occupy the road and ditches. The odor caused by withering leaves and explosives is very nauseating; the stink of dead bodies add to the disagreeableness.

On returning to Crezancy, we occupy the first empty billets we find. Morning finds us responding to the call for chow. Now I find myself assembled with the men left in my Company. Not one-third of the Company that crossed the Marne in pursuit of the Germans is with the Company now. Question after question is asked about several of the missing. I, for one, am not extremely grieved over the loss of anyone as I never before saw anyone in the Company. By good fate and my own resolutions, my crosses are not so heavy as a result of the outcome of the battles.

We remain in Crezancy, two days of which time I shall not go into many details. The French residents, now that the Germans have been driven back, are returning a few at a time to their demolished little city. They seem absolutely lost; and I do not doubt but that they are. Imagine yourself having everything you possess destroyed. Some roll a few belongings into the street upon wheel barrows. Some lead oxen and some wander aimlessly about. I am sure a hideous picture is before them as they come into the town.

While I sit on a piece of broken concrete, a lad of about twelve walks up to me and seems to gaze straight into my face. I am blind to his action until he tries to pronounce my name that he sees carved upon the front of my helmet. He says, "Heensaw," and gives a broad smile. He tries to sell me some cheese and I tell him, in my own language I have not seen a piece of money in so long a time that I doubt if I would know a coin if I should see it.

At the end of two days we are preparing to move out of the town. The Company has been replenished with recruits. Some of the men seem to think we are pulling out for Paris. However, they have not made many of us believe this story. We move out of Crezancy and for the third time cross the Marne, this time on a newly-constructed traffic bridge about seventy-five feet below where we crossed the pontoon bridge you have learned of previously. It is definitely known that the Germans have retreated about ten miles or about sixteen kilometers northeast of the Marne River in the direction of the Vesle River. Chateau-Thierry has for the last few days been evacuated by the Germans. It is generally thought that the Germans intend to retreat to the old Hindenberg line. The Hindenberg trenches have so far remained unbroken by the Allied Forces. Here it is thought they will stubbornly resist the American and French offensive. The American doughboys are rather enthusiastic over the fact that the enemy is on the run while only three days previous we ran a little.

Crossing the river, we load into trucks as many as they can pile in and take a most uncomfortable ride for at least three hours or more. In several spots along the road are to be seen pile after pile of shell hulls which evidence the fact that the Germans spent no little effort in trying to check our advance or smash our lines and forces into bits the night of the 14th and morning of the 15th in order that they might have an enjoyable walk into Paris. The surface features and general view of the country present hideous pictures. The Germans in their retreats leave nothing undestroyed. The battered and blasted buildings reflect on my memory to a picture of historical ruins.

French and American armored tanks move in great numbers in the direction of the enemies' positions. We travel several miles. It seems that the Germans have evacuated all of France. We finally unload, which is evidence that we are nearing the German offensive. German planes soar and hum high in the heavens. They are without question spying upon our movements. Some of the planes move in and out of heavy clusters of scattered clouds which seem to be perfectly still. Now large guns can be heard in the distance, a good indication that the enemy has mobilized its forces not so very far away.

Continuing our travel, battered houses, trees, roads, and the earth's surface present signs of intense warfare. The small towns through which we pass seem so void of life that to enter one of the houses finds one skittish as from a ghostly feeling.

We travel further and now the sun is almost setting. Presently we come into view of a fairly large town where we take up billets most of the night. The buildings are nearly torn down to make good shelter.

Before lying down, flares can be seen ascending in the direction of the Vesle River. Cannons are heard frequently from both the enemy and the allied batteries. The war clouds have again gathered and tomorrow shells, machine-guns, and rifle bullets will rain down upon us. Gas and shining bayonets will mix therein, and our shattered minds will again be entertained with the cruel and disgusting remembrances of the Marne. These hideous and distressing pictures of the ever-to-be remembered Marne are yet as vivid as the instant they were taking place. I for one can say that a heavy fear and dread rests heavily upon my mind. It seems that the dreadful and seeming inescapable struggles of the Marne would be enough for any one man to go through with. I am tired of it all and wish the sound of shells or bullets would never again disturb my mind.

23

Mixing It on
the Vesle [River]

Two hours before daylight, we are moving toward the enemy's position. The Germans are not retreating now. They mean to fight. Their artillery is heavily bombarding the road in front of us. Many shells are falling to our right and left also. Shrapnel sing close above our heads. The Germans seem to know we are on the road. Men are now screaming in front of us. A shell has lit among them. Some are no doubt killed and I know some are wounded. A shell lights not more than twenty feet to my right front. A man runs into the darkness screaming and carrying on terribly. He cries for help and says lots that I cannot understand. In fact, I do not try to grasp his words as I am in a confused state myself. A loud whistle is heard and someone I take for an officer gives the command to retreat back up the road. "The Germans are among us," someone mumbles. It is dark and I can see but very little; but you may rest assured I care not to meet any Germans anytime and of course much less at night. We come to a hill where we are pretty well out of danger of shell fire. Men dressed in American uniforms and who are generally thought to be American soldiers ask question after question. One of them asks me which state I am from. "Louisiana," I reply.

"What outfit are you with?" he asks. Remembering that we had all from time to time been instructed not to answer a question without certainty of knowing to whom we were talking, I decline to answer him. He storms at me bitterly saying, "I am an officer and want to know details."

I storm back saying, "It is funny an officer would come to a private to learn a few details when everybody's heads are about to be chopped with shells." He turns and disappears in the darkness. His every action convinces me that he is a German spy. Other men tell of similar incidents during this particular time.

Morning does not find us waiting to attack the Germans. Instead, we have established dugouts a short distance away on the side of a steep hill somewhat protecting us from shell fire. In the valley below several pieces of American and French artillery are located. It is fascinating to watch batteries operate. They jump a foot or two high on discharging the shell. The Germans drop shells in contempt to the fire of our batteries. An officer riding horseback drops from his horse when a shell lights and explodes close by him. The horse continues to run a short distance, then suddenly drops dead.

Four observation balloons float at high altitude further back than the artillery. They remind me of as many large elephants suspended in the air. Observation balloons do not move through the air at all. By means of strong cable they are connected generally with heavy tractors or trucks. They are adjustable at any desired height. Underneath the balloons are hung the observer's basket. These observers note the movements of the enemy and other facts of military value. There are nearly always two men with each balloon. One of the men notes the position of movements of the enemy by means of a map and calls same out to the other men who, by means of a telephone, conveys the information to the batteries. The balloons are often attacked by enemy planes and set on fire by means of machine-gun bullets that puncture them. The machine-guns are always used in an attack on a balloon. On seeing that their balloon is in the act of being destroyed, the observers thwart the efforts of the enemy to kill them by jumping from the basket and lowering themselves to the ground by means of parachutes.

Either side hates its enemy balloons intensely and, of course, are always eager to destroy them. So it happens right here that these four balloons I see in the distance are no exceptions. A German plane hums high above but not at all directly over our surroundings. The plane moves in and out of a curtain of clouds that overhangs the enemy territory. Seemingly the plane carries no interest in common. I have an idea that he has some balloons spotted and is waiting for the chance to attack. As I lie in my shallow dugout, I hardly ever take my eyes off the plane. It soars into the clouds and is lost to view. A few seconds later it reappears below the clouds. The motor does not hum any more. The plane coasts in the air. It comes in our direction. Gravity is all that moves it. I can see that it is trying to sneak up on the balloons. It comes closer and closer. When at about the same altitude as the balloon and approximately a hundred yards away, the plane begins to roar and a machine-gun fastened to the bottom wing opens up on one of the quartet. It continues to fly parallel with the rest of the balloons that are almost in a straight line and at the finish leaves them all burning masses of hydrogen. Eight men descend to the ground by means of parachutes and apparently are unharmed. The top surface of the ground on this hill is very sandy and loose. Two feet underneath the sand is a hard white clay that has almost the same appearance as blackboard chalk. It is hard to dig into and that is the principal reason our dugouts are so shallow here.

A large six-inch gun barks incessantly at the foot of the hill below. The powerful concussion at the discharge of each shell shakes the loose dirt and causes it to pour down upon my head. Before I realize it, I am grey-headed from carrying a head full of white sand. The shell discharged by the large gun is so large itself that it can be seen when it darts through the air between me and clear sky in the background. When first discovering a black streak that swished through the air, I could hardly believe it to be a shell. So I wait until the gun discharges again; again I see the same thing and call some other fellows' attention to it. They laugh at the idea of me imagining such a thing and it is with some coaxing that I finally succeed in getting them to take notice. When the gun discharged again, they gasped with surprise and summoned other men. Within a short time, twenty or more men lie with their eyes blared to get a glimpse of the lightning-like projectiles.

Another balloon floats high above us to the rear. It is not as far away as the other balloons were and has taken its lofty perch since the other balloons were destroyed. An hour or more after seeing it in the air, I notice that it shakes as if it is being brought toward the ground. The loud roar of an aeroplane motor abruptly disturbs the air, a machine-gun cackles and soon the balloon is a mass of flames. The observer leaves the balloon and descends toward the ground in his parachute. Now that the balloon has been destroyed, the German airman circles the parachute, doing his best to kill the man in it. An American machine-gun opens fire from a small cluster of bushes. He luckily brings the plane to the ground and the prisoner is evidently unhurt and unexcited. We crowd around him through curiosity. The man has reached the ground with his parachute and is now working his way through the assembly with a rifle in his hand. On coming in reach of the German, he brings the rifle down upon the airman's head with great force. The German flops upon the ground and struggles for breath several times. Blood spouts from his nose and ears profusely even after he gets on the road to eternity.

While we are in line for our small ration which consists of a slice of bread and some sweetened rice, a mule also helps himself to some hay directly below us at the foot of a small incline. When about half of the Company has been waited on, a shell can be heard approaching through the air. The men all scatter like a covey of quails and are soon lying flat. I figure one place is about as safe as another; therefore, I make a dive for the chow container and while I am rooting up my mess kit full of rice, the shell lands below and looking around at the same time it lands, I see the mule's neck and head torn off. The body is thrown back upon the ground and blood spouts from the amputation like a fountain of water.

By dark of this day, we have packs on our backs and everything ready to move on in the direction of the Vesle River across which we learn the Germans have taken positions. Flashes from our cannon decorate the surface in various spots; reflections from flashes from the enemy's cannons have the appearance of so many flashes of lightning as they drive the darkness away to the other side of the Vesle. Shells can be heard whining through the darkened air as they pass over; they can be heard falling short of us in the direction of the enemy lines. The flashes of the enemy shells can be seen piercing the darkness as the bombardment pours down upon the road leading in the direction of the river. We pull to the left around the main barrage and intersect the road between the shelling and the river. I am again and again reminded of the shelling on the Marne when the shrapnel and fragments harmonize in the air with their deathly threats.

On our way to the river, we pass through a rather high knoll through road that has been cut. There are several small dugouts that have been constructed at the juncture of the road and knoll. A fellow whose name is Clift and who is a new recruit and I occupy one of the dugouts. There must have been a bayonet engagement in the road at this point a few days previous, for there are both dead Americans and Germans in the road. The uniforms of most of the men are stiff with blood. The stink is very nauseating and some of the men adjust their gas masks in order to be able to endure it. One fellow lies in a puddle of blood. His uniform is very ragged and torn. It seems that his antagonist continued stabbing him after he fell mortally wounded. The bayonets that lie among the dead are still fixed and most of them are stained with blood. One of the dead's feet are amputated at his ankles. His shoes still hold his feet.

It not being a very dark night, the men keep close and do but little talking for fear that German patrolmen might find our location. Since I have taken up smoking, I take every opportunity to bum a cigarette or a stub. Procuring a cigarette from a fellow, I promise Clift he can have a few drags off of it. We hunker down in our dugout, conceal the light of the match with our helmets, light our cigarette, and take turn about in dragging off it. Clift holds his helmet over my face while I smoke a little and vice versa. He follows the smoking, which causes my large entrails to try to eat the smaller ones through telling about the good old juicy fried chicken his mother often times fixed for him back home.

"Gosh, Clift," I say, "If you don't shut up, you will have me out there searching those rotten bodies for a little corn willie and hard tack."

He laughs and says, "How would you like to have a few of those frying-sized roosters crowing in your belly?"

But he doesn't quit at that. He continues to torment me through describing those good old meeting dinners the churches so often pitch back in Arkansas. Before he finishes with his description, I can picture the preacher offing his hat preparatory to offering thanks for the most relishable long table of dinner ever to be spread under a grove of hickory nut trees.

Cannon balls that holler close above our heads cause us to seek our dugouts. The howl is so close above that we grow very restless. A mustard gas bomb that lights upon the embankment just above causes us to blare our eyes. But we do not adjust our masks until the gas spills down upon us, almost stifling me beyond breathing. My mouth feels raw and irritated. Lying with my mask on about fifteen minutes, I remove mine and sniff a little more. I immediately warn Clift that we are lying in a pool of gas and that we had best fan it out of the dugout. Fanning the gas out of our dugout by means of our blouses, we lie down again, a little later to be awoke with the most outrageous machine-gun fire I ever heard.

All night I have been confused with respect to the direction of the enemy and hence, thought them in opposite direction to what they really are.

It must be hard for you to understand why I got scared out of my breeches when about twenty American machine-guns opened up with a barrage on the embankment on the side of the road opposite the enemy lines. The flashes from the many guns almost light the road enough for the men to recognize one another's faces. Clift and I hunch each other through response to intense fear when the guns begin rattling over us across the road. He says, "We are gone this time."

Believe me, I am not found obstinate this time. I quite agree with him in as many words since I nurse the thought that those are enemy guns. Neither of us would give a nickel for our lives. We do not move other than tremble as though we are suffering with hard chills. Someone hollers, "Roll packs and get ready to move out quickly." I jump from the dugout expecting every second to be the last. My mind is reflected to the intense moments I experienced on the Marne. I manage to control my faculties enough to throw together most of my utensils and sling them into my pack. I grab my pack in one hand, rifle in the other and blunder down the road with the rest of the men. Most every man is moving, too. Even though he does not have his stuff in his pack, every fellow refuses to stay and roll pack under the center of excitement. Some of them carry their belongings under their arms and thrown over their shoulders. Some of them leave their helmets and rifles in their haste to get away and miss them when they are reminded that they are minus these most important implements.

Intersecting a railroad dump and track, and traveling by way of same awhile, we turn off into a forest. The German batteries begin shelling the swamp and again we are at the mercy of the heartless demons. When shells begin bursting, men begin mixing their screams with report of the bombardment. They are being chopped in two with fragments. Shells rain down all around, a repetition of the Marne. Machine-guns rattle in nearly every direction and bullets and shrapnel zip and squeal through the air as familiarly as ever. While running along a narrow path, I stumble over something large and soft. My rifle gets away from me in the fall and while I am fumbling and searching for it, a cannon shoots close by and the flash of fire finds my face not a foot from the smeared face of a dead man who lies across another dead soldier. The blare of the eyes and bloody face of the man on top leaves me with a feeling I cannot describe but will never forget.

Gaining my rifle and getting the run again, I am more than any time tonight pestered with bullets. A boy is fetched down in front of me and begs for someone to carry him out of danger. The man is unusually excited. He calls for his mother and says, "I'm dying."

Several shells drop among us. We take position on our bellies and draw our muscles into knots in response to the threats of the approaching shell. Some cannot lie still. They run from place to place to soon meet with a bomb that blows them up among the limbs. Feeling that one place is as safe as another, I hug the ground where I first fall. It is hard to do, however, and I feel like taking to my feet and running for life. A shell lands close to my rear and almost turns me a somersault. My feet feel numb and sting as though they were being gently pierced with many pins.

The order, "Forward, march" is heard in the darkness. The men begin to run fast ahead. I gain my feet and gladly follow. Shell fire yet spots the dark air with its flashes. I can hear men behind crying from being hit.

Our destination brings us into dugouts behind a railroad dump just across the river from the enemy. The earth is awake with machine-guns on the other side. The Champagne-Marne machine-gun nests do not exceed the number here. With the protection of the railroad, I feel so relieved from this den of hell.

The sky thunders with barking artillery and bursting shells. Machine-guns add to the harmony and loss of lives. The German batteries are littering the railroad dump and it seems that it will soon be blasted to the level of the rest of the ground. Flashes of fire spit through the darkness back in the swamp. It seems that a million bullets are whistling over us. We lie crouched in our dugouts like cowered pups trembling under the intense strain the hostilities cause us to nurse.

Shells pour down upon the track and pieces of rails and ties can be heard loudly fluttering upward into the dark air. Should one peek over the dump, his head would surely be chopped smooth off. My nerves are again becoming shaky and if this continues an hour longer, I am afraid I will suffer what is called "shell shock." Searchlights sweep the sky for planes. The planes more than likely soar preparatory to sweeping down upon balloons at daybreak. By means of the searchlights, the clouds and planes are more visible at night than during the daytime. It is now that I see a plane blinded by the extremely luminous searchlight. It must be at least a mile high. It reminds me of a candle fly fluttering around in the path of a car light as it tries hurrying out of danger by seeking hiding above some clouds nearby. Anti-aircraft guns try to bring the plane down but give up the attempt when the plane is swallowed by the clouds and lost to view.

Daylight drives darkness away. The shell fire and machine-guns have lightened up to some extent. The enemy must be waiting less threatening to try to discover the intentions of the Americans. But a river again separates the Americans and their enemy. There is no bridge to cross over on. I am glad there is not. Should we attempt it, the river would run red with our blood. The opposition is far too stiff this time to cross the Vesle. I should prefer swimming across at night than flirting with certain death to the amusement of the enemy. Let us pray that there will be a better and safer way of disposing of them than by first running the water off of the banks of the river with our dead bodies.

My canteen has long since been empty. I will eat that corned beef anyhow and it nearly drives me mad with thirst. I know there cannot be any water nearby. The knowledge of it seems to make me still more thirsty. I hear some canteens beating against one another, and coming out of my dugout, I notice a man has three in his hands filled with water. I ask him wherein he had such unusual luck. He informs me that there is a spring down a little way by the side of the railroad track but dangerous to get to. He says, "If you do not care much about your life, you might try getting some of it."

I do not make any reply; however, I know by the time he tells me where the spring is that I intend trying to get to it. By the time it takes me to get out of my dugout and get on the way, I am loaded with empty canteens. Every man would like to have his canteen filled but few will risk their chances in getting them filled. It sort of makes me angry to find that everyone wants his canteen filled at my risk. So I return all the canteens except those that belong to the men in my own squad. Taking care that I do not expose any of my person to the enemy over the dump, I finally run into the spring or rather a deep shell hole that resulted in a spring of water. In drinking I almost have to stand on my head. Filling my stomach to almost overflowing, I fill the canteens and get on my way back to my dugout. I notice several dead men lying in the grass nearby the track. It appears to me that this is my opportunity to replenish myself with corned beef; hence, I crawl out to the dead bodies and soon have their packs ransacked and my overcoat strutting with tins of beef and boxes of hard tack. A machine gunner spots me behind the track and opens up on me while I am returning from the dead bodies. Bullets cut the air close above me and taking position upon my belly, I crawl to the dump and proceed to my dugout. On reaching my earthly abode, someone says, "They like to have got him. Look at that bullet hole in his pack." To my own surprise, I take off my pack and find that it carries two holes, one on either side. A souvenir, I think, and if I live to reach home with this blanket, they will believe me when I tell it as I saw it on the front.

To our surprise, it has been rather an inactive day. There has been plenty of machine-gun fire but little shelling since about an hour after daybreak. The river separating us, neither enemy has been able to launch an attack. We, with the exception of a few thrills now and then, have enjoyed a quiet day of lounging behind the track. The most aggravating thing we have had to deal with today has been mustard gas that has been seeped up with the dew and now hidden in grass and shrubbery to burn and blister those who stir among it. Mustard gas seeks moist places and as a result several men are turning up blistered and burned under the arms, in the crotch, behind the knees, on the neck, etc. I am disappointed that I do not carry a small blister or burn as such is not generally detrimental but has its good effect in that it causes a fellow to get a rest and relief from the front.

When darkness again blankets the earth, we are relieved from the front by French soldiers. By midnight we are about five miles from the front. We are ordered to fall out for the night. Before retiring under my puppy tent, I wash my feet in some cold water in a brooklet and before I get back to my tent, I cannot speak above a whisper. Hence, the effect of the gas I breathed is telling on me.

24

The St. Mihiel Surprise

Three weeks have passed since we were relieved on the Vesle sector. Since leaving the Vesle, I have hardly been able to speak above a whisper. Everything has been quiet and peaceful these three weeks and we have gone so far as to drill a little now and then. We are supposed to be in Demange at the time I am writing now. New recruits have been assigned to the depleted Company. Some of them are very inquisitive about the front. One large and handsomely built fellow does not seem so concerned about what goes on up there and at the same time presents the appearance that he will give them his share of their trouble if he is ever offended by those Germans. I like him at first sight and his personality automatically prompts me to pick a conversation with him. I like him more and more all the time and I regret that he was not assigned to my squad as I would get to dugout with him when we go to the front again. His name is Harry McFerren. His home is in Bath, Michigan. We eat together at each issue of chow, bunk together here, take walks together, talk of our past together, and steal apple, plums and pears together.

During one of the days we occupy billets at this little town, I am charmed by a boy carrying sweet milk around trying to sell. I am yet ashamed to face the Company barber for not being able to pay him and hence, the same embarrassment prevents my purchasing any milk. But I figure out a plan by which I think I might get the milk anyway. The plan is to visit the barnyard before daylight and milk the cow before anyone is out of bed. So I get Bockleman, one of my squad, and before daylight we are consulting the cow as to the possibility of making a donation to our hungry tummies. Bockleman is to watch for civilians while I fill our canteens. The whole routine seems very funny to him and occasionally he laughs right out, causing me to tremble for fear we might be caught. The door to the stall is simple to open and soon I am inside telling Jersey to back her foot. Bockleman roars saying, "I know now you were raised in a barn." But Jersey is not so obedient and looking around and smelling of my arm, she begins acting any way but civil and I quickly leave her and her milk undisturbed. Bockleman, being a fellow who couldn't keep a funny joke, soon had everyone knowing that we had tried to steal some milk.

Bockleman and I were not to be so easily conquered. So the next night we try stealing some apples. In walking around, I had spotted an apple orchard in the enclosure of a high stone fence. The gate being locked, the only way to get inside was to climb over the fence. Well, the inviting apples over the top of this enclosure was enough to cause us to devise a plan quick. We planned that he would lift me on top of the fence and in turn I would pull him up so that he could help me out when we loaded our pockets with the contents. Using Bockleman for a stepping block, I gave a spring and landed upon top of the enclosure. Across the orchard from me sat another American on the fence. He says, "What are you doing here?"

"I am here for the same reason that you are here," I reply.

"Well, let's get going," he says.

Getting as many apples as we can carry, my partner and I decide that it might be best not to take all of them back to our billet. We hide them in a haystack and every night while in Demange we visit our fruit and have more pleasure as a result than any two fellows in town.

The morning of September the 12th finds us nearing the St. Mihiel Sector. The earth seems to be alive with artillery. The road we are on is a line of barking batteries. This must mean that the enemy is very strong. Anyway, we have been told all along this is expected to be the strongest point to crash.

Tonight we take up trenches. Tomorrow we will meet them out there somewhere. The sods of France will claim many of us on either side. Harry listens at the thundering barrage, turns and says, "It seems more like Hell than a war." I laugh. But not because I am tickled. I do it because I try and display some courage under such nerve-wracking excitement. Clift, who still retains the prize for most deliciously describing fried chicken, says, "I wish I were away from this ***** place and plumb back in Arkansas."

"Eating fried chicken, I guess."

"Yes! Eating more of Mom's good old fried chicken," he exclaims.

"There you go," I tell him.

"Yes, there I go. I wish since I have to die up here I could die full of good old fried chicken," he says.

"But instead," I say, "You will die with a belly full of diarrhea mixed with a little corn willie and hard tack."

We have hiked most of the night and it is now early morning. We are ordered to fall out until further instructions are given out. We are in a forest. Several of us unroll pack and make ready for a good rest. By the time I get my bed made and sprawled out, we are told to fall in. I snatch my equipment together as quickly as possible and move out with the Company.

The surface here has heretofore undergone an unusual amount of shelling and is extremely pitted and pimpled as a result. The road is full of craters filled with water for it has been and is still raining in slushes. The road is not hard-surfaced and from having been used extensively it is deep in mud and we bog all the way to our knees in walking through it. My pack feels like it will pull in two. My legs never before hurt so much under this unusual strain. I frown and scowl in putting everything I have left in my muscles to trudge on. The mama and sister-petted boy would have long since given up the hike. And by now some of those that have never been petted are giving up under the fatigue and falling by the wayside. I fall and weep because I feel that I am a nuisance by not being able to carry on like most of the others. The Company falls out for some reason or other about a quarter of a mile up the road and I finally make it to where it is. We rest for an hour or more and continue on.

Trees that stand near the road are muddy all the way to their tops. The explosions of shell that lit in the road are responsible for this.

The front linemen have for some time been over the top. They move forward while we follow up as reserve forces. A man on horseback lopes down the road. His horse is a solid mass of mud. A major stops him and asks him how it is all going up there. He replies by saying, "The Germans are running so fast we cannot catch up with them."

One guy evidently intending to furnish a little comedy says, "They must be coming this way if he is after them."

Shells fall aplenty up there. Machine-guns bark to the detriment of many. Bombs are ripping and tearing the earth to pieces judging from the sound of it all. The enemy must be centering their barrages upon the front linemen, for there are not many falling here. It sounds like they must all be falling up there.

The reports are now that 13,000 Germans have given themselves up and surrounded on a hill a little further up. The Company commander orders us to move on up toward the center of fighting. He smiles broadly. There must be good news sure enough. Guess he is pleased on hearing that as many Germans have given up. We are stationed close around the hill on which the Germans are supposed to surrender. By mid-afternoon, the prisoners begin coming down the road. I never saw so many Germans in my life. Two Americans are in charge of every two hundred Germans. Just to look at these prisoners, one could hardly help but believe the war must be over. At any rate, the St. Mihiel salient is completely wiped out. It has been a constant menace to the Allies since 1914. There are more German cannons taken here than I thought the Germans had altogether. The whole captured front is covered with them. Some are large and some are fairly small. Just the same they are cannons, the most dreaded monster used on the front. There are many machine-guns left by the enemy also. It seems like a complete victory for the Allies with little resistance from the enemy.

French civilians who were captured here in 1914 in a town cause grievances among some of the prisoners as they run down the road crying after them and holding on to their arms and wrists. The women and the prisoners they seem to seek weep loudly displaying unusual affection for one another. German prisoners stoop and kiss babes who are held by their mothers. An old man trodding along the road in civilian togs weeps loudly as if attending a funeral. Several pairs of men and women scream as if their burden of grief will kill them on being separated by soldiers. In most every case the couples are separated by force. Some of the German prisoners suffer being butted in the belly by rifles before they will agree to go on and leave their common-law wives and babes.

These women are said to have been serving as wives for German officers since their capture back in 1914.

Night finds us camping in the town these French civilians were taken from. While exploring the town, five fellows and I go into a cellar under what seems to have been an old hotel. On a table in the center of the cellar is a bottle of red wine and a glass beside it. One of the men reaches for the bottle and I storm at him not to touch it.

"Why?" he asks.

"It might be a mine," I reply. Agreeing that such might be the case, we all hurry out. Soon we are found in the orchard partaking of all the fruit we can find. While in the orchard, a terrific explosion takes place back in the center of town. The concussion of the explosion shakes us considerably. Stone and dust fill the air above the housetops as though it were being forced up by a geyser. Hurrying back to town, we find that the whole end of the hotel has been blown away. We are convinced it is a mine sure enough. Since a few men are missing from the Company, it is logical to believe they met death in the blast.

We remain on the St. Mihiel front four days. We do no fighting at all as the enemy has completely called it quits on this sector. I shall write a few descriptions of different features of the front here after which I will move on to Mense-Argonne.

Trenches of the St. Mihiel Sector look old and are from four to six feet deep. A big portion of the trenches is concreted and sheltered. The Germans undoubtedly were sure they were in for a long stay when they made such constructions. Some of their dugouts are fifteen feet deep and strongly protected from powerful bombs by being covered with huge mounds of dirt and logs. Some of these deep dugouts are well fixed with household fixtures. I am speaking from my experiences of two of these dugouts which I explored. Here occupancies are found of card tables, small pianos, looking glasses, demijohns, cots, several tins of canned meat, and a few playing cards and cigarettes scattered over the floor. Entering one of these dugouts, it actually seems that we had suddenly closed the doors on the debaucheries of Hell and stood face to face with at least a degree of civilization. This is only momentarily though so far as ease of mind is concerned. For emerging from the dugouts, we again gaze upon hideous pictures of cratered planes and forests and towns rendered worthless by the greedy German forces who tried stubbornly to take all France and rip and tear it all the way to the earth's center. It seems that the restoring of France is beyond the power of human skill and labor. It seems that a power, a super power, dominating all natural obstacles is the only one capable of restoring France to fifty percent of her original wealth and beauty.

Large guns that composed the powerful German artillery stand hidden from aeroplanes by means of camouflages. About two feet of the guns protrude through a hole in the screen. The American attack was so sudden and strong that the Germans did not have time to save their artillery in their retreat or before they were taken prisoners. The huge shells stacked around them look to be sufficient to blast France in two.

It seems that Germany should be licked now. She has lost so much in this drive that the Americans take renewed courage. They behave as though they just know the war is over. However, before you finish reading "As I Saw It on the Front" you will think it has hardly begun.

Since we, I mean my Company, had no action on this sector, we are greatly pleased but surprised. I shall not hold your mind here any longer. From now on, you will read it as I saw it on the Meuse-Argonne front.

25

Waiting in Reserve

September 17th finds us having been transferred to the Meuse-Argonne forest front. There is not much of a forest here now. It has been almost completely destroyed by artillery fire during the past four years. We are not held on the front lines yet. We are moving up in reserve. The country here is crude-looking. It surrounds Verdun where the most terrific shell fire that ever fell was laid down in the early years of the war. Over 500,000 Germans were killed here during the first two years of the war to say nothing of those killed by the Germans. The ground here is pulverized and pitted. The surface is nothing short of a curtain of craters. I have not yet seen anything that will come close to comparing with this be-haggard country. The surface is covered with dewberry vines. Limbs lie thick underneath the vines and mixed in the ground. While picking berries, if one is not careful he will suddenly step off into a hole that will swallow him beneath the vines. Every tree has been blasted and torn beyond any use except, perhaps, for fire wood. No matter how far one might look, the distance does not reveal a whole tree. The trees remaining are scarred and chopped to such an extreme extent that it is hard to find a spot unhit large enough to place a finger upon. Some of the haggard stumps hold fragments so deeply embedded that a heavy weight could be suspended upon them. I find this to be true when I pull my weight upon one of the steel splinters. There is almost no life in nearly all the riddled stumps. Once in awhile, a few green leaves can be seen sticking on a stump. While constructing dugouts here, we remove about as much steel as dirt. It is the most devastated territory by far I have seen previously on the front.

This is a lonely place except for the report of guns, barking of machine-guns in the distance and humming of aeroplanes. It is impossible to find a level spot to lie down upon. Those who desire level places must make them by means of their shovels. There is no battlefield in France that has lain under so long a siege of terrific fighting and bombardment. Here in 1916, was the principal scene of fighting.

Night comes on and finds us crouching in our newly constructed little dugouts. When I closed my eyes to slumber, the sky was clear and starry. Within thirty minutes' time I am interrupted by rain drops beating on my face. I am forced to pitch my pup tent with another fellow or else lie in mud which is not infrequent up here I am sure. The wind whistles from the north and we lie exposed to our first cold and chilly winter weather. Rain drops slip down heavily upon the tent while my mind suffers with the thought of all of it we still have to endure during the winter in the muddy and icy trenches.

The next day we travel further in the direction of the front. It is a zig-zag affair while we travel along. The whole line of men move as though they were walking upon the waves of a windy ocean. The cold rain pours down, filling the many small craters and soon we are wet from foot to ears and present the appearance of walking mud-dummies. The men cannot move along in constant motion. The procession is so long that the line is thrown into congestion causing the men to move in waves.

During this same hike, the men are ordered to fall out. Even though the rain does fall in slushes, most of the soldiers try to find some place to sit down in order that their feet can get rest. Harry and I notice some waterproof dugouts near the road and seek covering there. On entering the dugouts, it seems very warm and inviting. But after being in there awhile, we begin shaking again and find it colder than if we had remained in the rain.

Our destination for the day finds us falling out in a forest that is not nearly so ragged and devastated as the one in which we stayed last night. It is several miles removed from the scene of forest I described above. What battle markings there are here, however, are mostly fresh, showing that this has been the scene of recent fighting.

On falling out, several men stir in the search for food they might be able to find as such is usually the case where recent battles have been fought. Some build fires in order to warm and dry by. While warming by a fire, a man finds a piece of an old hand grenade and not thinking it to be dangerous tosses it in the fire. The result was one man killed outright and three wounded.

The men who went in hunt of food return with plenty of beef and hard tack. They inform us who didn't go that about a half mile beyond the forest is an open field that contains plenty of dead Americans and Germans and that a few of them have some tins of beef on their bodies. This story interests Harry and me and we are soon on the hunt for the dead. We find plenty of dead all right, but only a few tins of beef.

A new recruit who has recently been assigned to the Company and who is certainly ignorant of the significance of all the actions of the old trenchmen becomes inquisitive about so many men taking walks off into the bushes all the time. A kind of an old and disgusted-looking fellow answers by saying, "When you have been up here long enough to have nothing in you but a belly full of corned beef and diarrhea, you will understand why we go to the bushes so often."

To me, this being the best comedy yet on the front, I sprawl back upon my back and laugh until my sides are sore. From this time on, I often ask the new recruit if he yet understands why so many men have to take walks. On one occasion he replied by saying, "Yes, I am getting to where I am about to understand. Last night I ate a big bite of that old corned beef and then drank a canteen of cold water and was taking walks all night."

During the four days we stay here in the forest, there is nothing much to do except stroll around so long as we keep under cover. When we are not strolling about, we usually congregate in various groups and talk of things back home, about the front, and about this, that, and the other. A lot of the men like to brag about their parents and especially every man gets a kick out of boasting about what a great man physically his father has been or is yet. One man says, "My father has never had the toothache but once in his life."

I say, "That's nothing. My father is rubbing sixty years and hasn't got an unsound tooth in his head."

A fellow speaks up and says, "That's saying a whole lot all right. You mean he ain't got an unsound tooth in his mouth?"

"Not a one," I say. "He had them all pulled out a few years ago."

I feel kind of proud of my joke being that everyone responded with a heavy roar or guffaws.

A few days after stopping here, the north wind gives way to a hot sun that warms things up again. We are all thankful for the mild weather, too, as it is so disagreeable to lie on the cold ground with nothing much between us, but it is so warm now that the stink from the dead bodies is again stirring in the air and is being carried to us by the wind that comes from the direction of the decaying slain. One guy writes a letter home, says, "I guess they will smell this scent of the dead ones on my letter when they read it."

Most all the men complain of the rotten odor and some of them threaten adjusting their gas masks in order to be able to get a decent breath. I try to be more reticent as I had rather be bothered with a disagreeable odor than be bothered with a thousand machine-guns and cannons further up.

We are now passing our fourth day here. It is afternoon and I propose to someone that we go in search for some food in the forest instead of the field beyond the forest. He agrees and we spend some time loitering around in the woods. We find a good many dead men, mostly Americans. It looks as if there has been no attempt to salvage the dead. It seems that all minds are concentrated on smashing the German stronghold and paving the way to a quick cessation of hostilities. It is easy to tell that the Americans have been on the advance all the time but with a heavy loss of men. I am able to count about one dead German to every ten dead Americans. The Germans have been strictly on the offensive and for the greater part with the use of machine-guns. The woods we are in are spotted with machine-gun nests that have been overcome by the brave Americans. Dead gunners are found by some of the machine-guns. Dead Americans are found sprawled upon the ground or hanging over a mass of thick underbrush. I see only one Frenchman that has been slain. His body is in a bullet-proof tank that has been disabled by a bomb. Of course the Frenchman was killed the same time the tank was disabled. Through curiosity, I open the door to the tank and receive a gush of the rotten odor in my face that causes everything in my belly to act as though it were going to cause me to heave it up. My short glance of the interior reveals a one-pounder situated on one side of the tank and a machine-gun on the other. The dead body's face and hands were black with a long period of decay.

Continuing my exploration, I meet a surprise. I never thought a human body contained so much blood until now. A German whose head has been blown partly off lies head foremost on the side of a railroad dump. In a hole at the foot of the dump his blood has puddled and coagulated. There seems to be at least four gallons of it. Green flies literally cover the body and blood. The mangled head and pond of blood are already a mass of rolling maggots.

It looks that there has been no attempt to salvage the dead. All minds are concentrated on smashing the German stronghold and driving the way to quick cessation of hostilities. Let us pray that it all ends tomorrow and that we will be acting preparatory to taking a boat home where we will be welcomed with arms and not machine-guns and cannons; and let us pray that we will never have to advance or run from these dastardly bullets and bursting cannon. Even the thought of machine-guns and shrapnel bullets zipping by my head makes my blood run cold and my heart thump and squish my blood through my neck veins.

Midnight finds us lying crouched in our dugouts or lying upon the surface. Shells begin howling through the dark air with the sound of lonesome dogs. A few of them land close by. A single bomb drops from the air and salutes by landing in an old dead and seasoned beech tree. Its fragments and shrapnel bullets spread in every direction. Several men were sleeping under the tree. Three of them will never see the sun rise again. Some scream and cry from wounds. One of the wounded makes himself conspicuous and opening his blouse reveals that he has been ripped to the hollow and his entrails spill out the opening. He is bloody to his ankles. The entire throat of one of the dead men is torn away, leaving his neck bone plainly exposed.

It looks that we might stay here another night. Funny thing—the enemy does not shell here some more, at least. Guess they have too hard a time keeping those on the front lines entertained. But there is no telling when a million of these dreaded devils will pour down upon us riddling everything into ribbons. The same shell kills two mules.

Daylight finds us getting ready to move further back. This action causes most of us to decorate our faces with smiles. It is always a pleasure to travel in opposite direction from the lines and in the event anyone tells you he likes to face guns and fight an army of soldiers, there is just one reply you should make and that is, "Ah, baloney."

Our destination brings us to a stop on a hill near Verdun. My first attraction is a few wounded men carving pictures and etc. on one-pounder shell hulls. Their efforts are to bring them a few francs. One of the carvings is exceptionally attractive. A lieutenant offers the owner five francs for it. He refuses. He then offers him ten francs, which the wounded man refuses. The officer says, "Ah, that's enough," and throws down ten francs in his lap. The man begs the officer to return his shell hull as he wants to take it to his mother when he returns to the United States. The officer bawls him out and walks on.

It being the custom for the men to dig-in, we most automatically do so and to our surprise, find bones and pieces of clothing of men who were buried here more than two years ago. The first bones that I dig into are a few bones of a human foot. I immediately change my point of digging; but to no avail, for the next place I dig-in, I find more bones. This time I dig right on and soon have a shallow dugout surrounded by a display of bones. Several of the men seem to get fun out of their uncovering. I get no fun, however, but feel the effects of spooks during the late hours of night.

Remaining here for several days, we are informed that we will move back toward the lines to be held in close reserve for the next engagement. This does not touch any of us in the right spot. We draw long-faced figures; some look as though they had just had the death sentence read off to them. I say "they"; I really should say "we."

The sun is now being swallowed beyond the horizon. We move toward the front. I feel that our few peaceful days are to be spoiled by the belching flashes of Hell not long off. An hour more finds us moving under a blanket of darkness. In the morning at daylight, we will be slung out into view as prey for the unmerciful enemy who relishes our flavor. In the morning we will try to trudge along under a mass of spouting geysers while they spread a blanket of craters upon the surface in their greedy effort to mangle our flesh with the sods they so wish to conquer and call theirs.

26

Visitation to Hell

Before midnight, the American artillery begins slowly challenging the enemy to come on and fight. The enemy keeps very quiet. They are good to us. They do not wish to harm us yet. They are so modest that they are uneventful. Our artillery pours down upon them but still they make no reply. The enemy is sure to be hugging mother earth very affectionately right now. They will continue to hug her until the chance is ripe to lay us forever upon the bosom of the dear old mother.

By midnight the American batteries are flashing everywhere in the rear. We lie in front to go over and see what they have done in the morning. The guns can be seen flashing through the woods we now occupy. They can be seen flashing as far to the right and left as our eyes will permit us to see. The flashing daggers pierce the darkness by the thousands. The vacuums keep the air in a mad uproar.

The front linemen will go over in the morning at 4 o'clock. We will follow if they advance. Anyway, there will be a fight; a big fight. If the front linemen fail on their objective, we will be right in the middle of the big rumpus. I feel that morning will bring more sides to the real test.

Daybreak finds cannon and machine-gun telling it more vociferously than ever. The German batteries are resenting madly. Shells fall like rain. The enemy is upon us. Dirt is thrown in the air and rains down upon us as true repetition of the Marne. We move on in the midst of it all. This is suspense that many of us cannot endure all day. My ears are already beginning to ring from the bangs of the enemy shells that disturb them every second. An extremely white cloud of smoke rises in the direction of the front lines. It cannot be the smoke from shell explosions. It must be a smoke screen to shield the advancing men, whoever they might be. The American artillery roars like a million blasts of dynamite in a minute's time. Our batteries are tearing them to pieces and they are tearing us to pieces. Men screaming in agony can be heard behind the spouting geysers. They roll and tumble at the explosion of the enemy bombs. Long-range bullets stray about us. We cannot hear the enemy machine-guns. The explosives' reports drown them out. A shell lights by a fellow, tearing him into ravels. Blood spatters upon our uniforms and faces. Again a devil bellows down upon us, playing havoc with several men. Some run here and thither. Some are dead; some are dying. A shrapnel che-e-ows so close to my head that I think to duck after it has passed on.

Four Frenchmen operate a cannon to my left. They fire three or four times in succession, then turn to a demijohn of wine and drink while the bombs threaten to tear their heads off every second.

The American infantrymen move in hordes. The wounded accompany the explosives as they bang down among us sending their splinters and shrapnel bullets into our uniforms. The German airmen fly above the mass of moving Americans, doing everything possible to stop them by tearing them in two with hellish bombs. Everywhere one looks shells pour down by the hundreds. If one lives through this he should know it is by the guidance of a Supreme. A shell lights a few feet from a man. It tears his head off, rolling it upon the ground like a ball. Blood squirts from his neck like water from a broken hose. Those still afoot move on, crouching under the mass of geysers. Every man looks as though he expects to be torn in half every second. Dublinsky now lies on the ground mortally wounded. His blouse is torn open and his entrails spill out the opening. He begs for a drink to quench his thirst before he gets on the road to the country removed from this one. His entrails are a mass of blood. The excitement is all that keeps him alive any time. He stains his own hands through trying to put his entrails back into his belly. He weakens; slumps, and then dies.

A German and an American lie facing each other with a bayonet rammed through each. The German bayonet protrudes all the way through the American's body while the American's bayonet seems to have gored the German half its length. This is my first evidence of a hand-to-hand engagement.

The earth already scarred beyond recognition is still being churned by the Germans' bursting shells. Hardly a level spot a foot square can be found. The earth's surface nurses a million wounds right in this vicinity. Men lie ground into mince meat. Some dead bodies have already been completely covered up by shell flipping dirt over them. Some of the dead bodies were chopped to pieces long after life became extinct. Some lie partially covered up with dirt slung over them by the barrage. Some lie half covered with water in the bottom of large shell holes. An American's body, lifeless for several days, presents a terrifying and hideous picture as it lies across a pack with its head drawn back and maggots rolling like a white ball in each eye socket.

A man terribly frightened runs with blood pouring from his mouth as a result of a shrapnel bullet tearing a large hole under his right eye. He tries to talk but only jabbers and cries. His tongue is evidently badly torn. Men still lie amidst the barrage screaming and calling for someone to help them. Occasionally, I get a glance of Harry when my eyes are brought off the ground from expecting the next bomb to put my lights out. Harry does not seem very much excited. He walks leisurely along as the earth rocks under the heavy downpour of bombs. The whole earth seems to be mad as splinters and shrapnel scream from its bosom trying to take every man's head from his shoulders. Glancing to my left I see a bomb light directly in front of a man, killing him and sending his rifle whirling into the air. Almost at the same time an American's big gun is smashed with a bomb and its ammunition exploded. The earth shakes under the explosion. Shell hulls, smoke, and dirt form a dark cloud where the ground and the men run madly when the mass of waste begins showering down on the ground. The men refuse to advance under the heavy rain of bursting bombs. They take shell holes for protection. I flop into a small one. I know it is of little use for protection but just anything is inviting when one's life is threatened every second. I do not tremble as much as when it all first began. I guess I am getting tamed to it as it goes on. I do not lie in my shell hole long until a large shell shakes the earth about fifty yards from me. Smoke and dirt throw a black screen over the point of explosion. A large black object races across the ground like a big rabbit. It comes directly toward me. Fearing that it would hit me, I throw my hobnail up to block its force. Before I realize what took place my head is knocked back between my shoulders by my knee that got its force from the heavy ball of steel which was the nose of a burst shell.

A shell falls almost upon me. It shakes me severely and nearly covers me with dirt. Another shell lights close by sending a man rolling over and over. The fallen victim stops near me. I notice that his blouse is torn badly in the back. He groans like a helpless beast. He struggles for breath. His back is ripped all the way into his lungs and the air he breathes whizzes from the wound. He begs pathetically for water while the G.I. cans continue to threaten every one of us and spew dirt upon every man.

Gas bombs have begun to fall. The gas sneaking from the shells fall undermindedly in the grass. The explosions and concussions from the shells whip into the air and soon the gas is taking quarters with us in our holes. I adjust my mask quickly. Soon my view is hindered by the mist that collects on the eyepieces. My face is a running stream of sweat and it is most impossible to keep my glasses clear.

As I view it, death is making monkeys of us and flirting in the faces of all the men.

A doughboy comes running up the hill. A gas bomb lights directly in front of him. The gas gushes into his face. He drops instantly dead. Shells continue to tear through the air with terrific force. The earth trembles when they light. A forest to our right is being bombarded severely. There is not so much shelling here now. It seems that most of the cannons have focused their guns upon the woods up there. Smoke and dust boil over the treetops, presenting the picture of a forest fire. Men run from the woods out into the opening. It is just more than they can stand. They seek a safer place. Someone screams to my rear. The victim gains his feet and passes nearby. He holds his hip. A shrapnel bullet or splinter has carved itself upon the soldier.

There is practically no bombing going on right here now. The shelling seems to be centering on a hill oblique from this point and in the woods to the right. German prisoners have begun passing by in small and large groups. They seem fairly cool and the expressions upon their faces reveal anything but dissatisfaction of their capture. They seem interested and stirred only when a shell drops among them, killing one and slightly wounding others. These prisoners are good evidence that the Americans have made at least a progress in taking their objective.

Realizing that almost all danger has passed here with respect to shell fire, I perch upon my haunches for a little relaxation. I see Harry rolling a cigarette. He wastes none of his tobacco. He must still possess a steady nerve. The captain is also still alive.

A fellow coming out of his shell hole looks at me, smiles broadly and asks, "How goes it?"

I reply, "All right I guess so long as I can come out of it with my apparatus working well."

A man passes close by with his hand bleeding. "What are you going to say?" I ask.

"It's Hell on the front," he replies.

This means they are fighting like heck I know. It is not all over yet. I can hear their rifles and machine-guns barking up there. We who are here had better be thankful, I guess. Maybe tomorrow we will follow them up. We will riddle and be riddled. Hideous pictures can be imagined.

The sole of my foot still burns and throbs. But how lucky am I to be able to sit here whole and look upon the pulverized earth with maybe a chance to live on through it all. How fortunate would I be to live through it and when out of it, write about it giving those who never smelled the deathly odor or heard the deathly threats a picture of how men have to suffer and to die for the cause of the country in which they live; how they have to fight to keep men of other countries from hogging their land and embarrassingly subduing them. It seems cruel that we should have to stay up here in mud, lice, shellfire, and machine-gun fire and fight for something no matter what it is. How cruel it all may be, we would rather die here than let the Germans pass among our live bodies smiling victors.

On the hill to my right, where the shelling is so excessive now, a man is seen running amidst the falling bombs. It is too bad for him, as death has him hand-cuffed and is leading him to the gallows. The man runs with face covered with his hands. A large bomb lights under him and for a second he is concealed by the smoke and dirt; then above the smoke it can be seen that his body has been torn in two. His hips and legs whirl rhythmically above the curtain of the smoke and debris.

A doughboy running fast from the woods stops and asks, "Where is the dressing station?"

His face is heavily covered with blood and his blouse is stiff in front with it. He does not seem the least bit excited which accounts for the fact that courage is rare among the boys.

It is now well on in the afternoon. I suggest to some fellows that we go down the hill and see if we can find some corned beef on the several dead that have been killed by the barrage down there. We go and in a few minutes have plenty of tins of corned beef. Here in a few spots the grass is as stained with blood as though beefs had been butchered upon it. Most of the men are torn beyond recognition. One of the dead lies with legs so broken and twisted that they take a very ugly shape. Believing that I recognize this body, my blood runs cold and I gasp with surprise. The rear of his head and neck look exactly like that of my brother Patrick's. I quickly turn him upon his back. His face is so smeared with blood that it does no good in helping me learn the truth about the body. I wipe the blood from the dead man's face; I open his mouth. It is full of blood. Remembering that my brother's fingernails were long and narrow, I grab the cold hands, examining them with haste. I stand astride the dead body and wipe sweat from my brow while my heart resumes its natural gait from my mental satisfaction that the dead man's body is not that of my own blood.

The forest and hill to our right are yet being bombarded with the courage of savages. The bang of the shell upon the hill and woods is so bombastic that it seems they would quake under the force. The fragments and shrapnel keep music through friction with the air. It seems that all the tiniest insects would be dead by now.

The air still wheezes through the torn lungs and back of the man near my dugout. He begs for water as his voice grows weaker. I turn him upon his back and give what little water I have left in my container. His lips are as white as cotton. He is slowly dying. He begs for first aid but knowing I cannot make a worthwhile application, I secure the aid of another man and we carry him back a little way and leave him, a certain victim for eternity.

26. Visitation to Hell

Returning to the hill, I find the men digging in. I start to work on my shell hole and soon have a fairly decent-looking dugout. I lie down outside of my earthly abode and whistle for Harry to come over and talk and smoke with me, it being understood he is to furnish the smoking tobacco. He comes accompanied by another man and we all talk and quiet our nerves with clouds of smoke. We are suddenly interrupted by a squadron of German bombing planes that come roaring low down, dropping bombs upon the hill and scaring us terribly. Harry and the other men being closer than I to my dugout, they flop into it ahead of me, leaving me hugging them with my back and pack exposed above the surface. The birdmen fly away while a hundred or more shots are taken at them. We crawl lazily out. "It was always a pleasure for anyone to visit my house whole," I tell these two gents. "But," I say, "if you have to visit to my ill effect any more you can stay away."

They roar with laughter and I roar with them. I point to a man who is being dragged out of a hole terribly torn and say, "I could have as easily been in his shoes."

Harry's friend reaching in his pocket for some smoking says, "Ah, let's all forget and smoke again."

We talk awhile longer and I get up to go down to the foot of the hill and fill my canteen. No sooner than my back is turned to them they set up an awful roar of laughter. I turn around and say, "What is the matter with you durned pranks anyway?"

They slap their thighs and laugh so that I really become somewhat offended. When they have laughed until their sides hurt, they inform me that my pack is terribly torn. Taking it off, I find that part of my pack and mess-kit have been ripped by a fragment from one of the serial bombs. The mess-kit is torn nearly in two and my spoon, knife and fork are ruined.

A first lieutenant becoming aggravated at our moving about too much, yells, "Get down and stay down. Can't you guys see that we are all victims to hell?"

27

A Few Incidentals

The Allied planes must feel that the Germans have supremacy of the air. The German planes growl like stubborn bulldogs while the Allied planes soar off a distance seemingly afraid to venture close. While the enemy have generally proven inferior on the ground, they have for the greater part held supremacy in my presence.

One of the principal thrills here is the chasing of an American plane by three German planes. Machine-guns bark from the planes while the chase pursues The American plane, becoming disabled, begins to wobble and soon after comes to the ground.

An American airman becoming eager for battle casually flies right into a cluster of German planes, only to be brought down before the fight gets under good headway. Walking over to the scene of the tragedy, the dead man lies covered with canvas and other debris.

Other planes quarrel at one another with machine-guns. But they take pretty good care not to venture too close. In the event Germans venture toward the Allied planes, the latter satisfy their desire by hunting distant quarters. Should the American and French planes equal the Germans' machines in number, the results would be different.

Both sides are trying to bombard each other's planes with anti-aircraft guns. The timed bombs cluck incessantly around the planes and there high above, a plane Allied or German, I cannot tell which, bursts into flames. It roars to the ground, leaving a lane of smoke behind. This just about climaxes all the aerial stunts I see here today.

It is late in the afternoon now. I am more than thankful that I have been spared from the unmerciful enemy's claws. I have tried to tell most everything that happened that I thought you would be interested in. I did not see but just a little compared with all that happened. It is impossible for one man to see one-half of that which happens even close to him.

Night comes on and I am on patrol duty. Eight of us walk quietly out of our territory, past the line of trenches confronting the enemy trenches. We are led by a second lieutenant. No one dares light a cigarette, or mutter a word; no one should even break a stick lest a machine-gun opens up on us riddling us with bullets. A star-shell far back in the enemy's side finds us crouching upon the ground scared to trembling that we will be seen. What if we should? We would be killed surely. Entering upon no-man's land, we crawl and sneak along as though we expected every second to be the last upon this earth alive. We come to a weeded section. We crawl. Our necks and bellies become painful. Our arms seem that they will break in two. No one says a word. We are out to spy upon the enemy and if we make the least bit of noise they will put an end to it all. My rifle is aggravating to carry since I am compelled to crawl upon the ground. A bush sometimes shakes; then everyone says, "Sh-h-h." We keep crawling. The man just in front of me hunches my arm and says, "Be quiet; Germans. Pass it on."

I touch the man behind me and pass the word to him. Everybody lies as quiet as mice. Should the Germans see or hear us they will trounce upon us with bayonets and gore us through and through. I lie quiet. I listen. I raise my head and look in front to see that we are nearly overlooking a steep bluff below which the Germans are located. I can hear them muttering and laughing. My heart thumps audibly. Maybe they know where we are and are surrounding us to take us prisoners or have a lot of fun out of us. The man in front of me hunches me again. He says, "Face to the rear and crawl quietly back. Pass it on." I pass it on and soon the man behind becomes the man in front of me and we are crawling with the ease of as many snakes. We are soon out of danger of them and reporting back to the Company. The lieutenant reports the find to the batteries and shells bang down upon the enemy we find.

After returning from no-man's land, we take up dugouts for the night. A fellow whose name is Cox occupies my dugout with us. Cox is an enthusiast on religion and physiology. He is devoutly Christian and would have everyone know it. He often quotes scripture when out of the range of shell and bullets and prays like all the rest of us when he is a possible prey to them. He takes special delight in tracing the blood through the body. He never indulges in any dirty talk but always talks clean and would prefer everyone else do the same way. Someone asks him if he has become such a clean gentleman and devout Christian since coming to the front or has he always been that way. He says, "I've been that way ever since I was quite a boy."

I am very sleepy and tired and would like to drop off to sleep and not awake for twenty-four hours. Cox being very talkative, however, will not allow me to go right off to sleep. By the time he gets good and stretched out, he says, "Well! It's been a mighty touchy and nerve-wracking day sure as you were born, hasn't it?"

"It sure has," I answer.

"Well," he says, "we ought to be mighty thankful that we got through alive."

My eyelids feel like they weigh ten pounds when I try to raise them in response to answering Cox. He talks on a little longer and says, "Suppose we have a few words of prayer before we drop off to sleep?"

I say, "That is all right but you had better make it snappy or I'll be asleep before you get through."

He begins. I try to be unrude and stay awake. He keeps it going and going. I feel myself growing impatient. Getting straightened out on a few long, drawn-out sentences, he lowers his voice and mumbles for several seconds that almost find me snoring by the time he finishes. But every time just before I grab for the last link that would have meant solemn slumber for me, Cox pitches his voice all the way out of the dugout and into the other dugout. My eyes blare open as if in response to the approach of a shell. He pulls this one on me three times and I become too wrought up. The fourth time he jarred the air with the high pitch of his religious voice, I punch him in the side and say, "Cox, bring that to a close. You have already prayed enough for everybody at the front." He whispers awhile longer and I hear him say, "Amen."

"Thank God," I think.

Before daybreak, our sleep is interrupted by the command, "Outside and roll packs."

Never before had I despised this command so much. I was sleeping well for one time. Now I am interrupted and will have to give up the best nap yet to get on the front.

Getting on the move, we find that we are moving in opposite direction to the enemy lines. We learn that we are moving back to evade heavy shelling that is expected at daylight. Before going far, shells begin coming over a few at a time. Their flashes pierce the darkness where they fall.

Men suffering intensely from the effects of diarrhea are forced to fall out risking themselves to any number of shells that might fall any minute. I notice one unfortunate fellow taking siding with nothing on but his birth robe. He uses his underwear for a towel. The wind whistles from the north. So it is hard to tell which is more terrifying: the wind, shells or diarrhea.

The end of our destination finds us constructing dugouts on the side of a very steep hill. The purpose of the hill is to protect us from shell fire. The bottom of my dugout is bumpy and hard with stones. My hip bones have already begun to feel sore and irritated from lying on the ground so long. And now they feel sorer than ever. Before now, I have been able most of the time to make a depression in the ground for my helmet in which I would put the undershirt and have a pretty nice pillow. But now my helmet rocks upon the stones and soon I sling it out of the dugout and see only the undershirt and a pair of drawers for my "heading," as I call it. Harry makes all kinds of fun of that word "heading" saying he never heard the substitute for a pillow called "heading" before. I tell him that is the word we Southerners use when speaking of something to lay our heads on and that we do not sleep well if we do not say "heading."

We remain on this hill several days. Two men are killed during our stay here. A shell slid down the hill one night and caught them napping. The name of one of the men is Bacon. I can always remember his name by associating it with the bacon we like to eat.

The last night we are on the hill the Germans shell immensely. Shell- fire almost keeps darkness driven from the earth down in the valley. I am very nervous all night. I guess it is because I know we are to take up trenches at daylight. I flounce and jump when a shell squeals by. In the event the sound of one catches me napping, I almost jump clear out of my dugout. Everyone dreads the coming of tomorrow for they know it means going over the top. I cannot make up my mind that I will be able to stand all that shelling and shooting again to say nothing of the thousands of chances

of getting killed. It is tormenting to one's mind. Do not let anyone tell you that it is not. Yell "Baloney" if they try to make you believe any such "bunk" that a man does not care for facing any enemy up here even if he is weak.

During the night I am certain I hear someone holler "roll packs." I get out and before I fail to notice that no one else is stirring, I have my pack nearly rolled. I am surprised beyond words. I ask if someone did not say "roll packs." Some guy evidently disturbed by my actions yells "Get to hell back in your dugout and stay there until you are told to roll pack, for you will be up there to get killed soon enough."

"Well!" I think. "All I can make out of it is that I have experienced a hallucination."

28

In Hell Again

The coming of daybreak finds us lying crouched half-side deep in water in dugouts just a little way back of the front line trenches. It is compulsory that we suffer this exposure lest we are mowed down by machine-guns. Rain still pours down and I try to make up my mind that it might be best to stick my head outside the dugout and let a bullet climax my agony. But no; one will cling to the last straw through effort to save his life.

I feel cheap cowered here under the threats and bang of the tormenting enemy. I wish I knew we were doing all this for the right and just cause; I wish I knew for sure we were lying here freezing and nursing the dread and mental worry of going over for something that it is worthwhile doing it all for. Are we fighting a political war? Are we lying here almost dying through the influence of some or more financial wizards that crave more and more millions even at the cost of us being blown into atoms? I think of the encouragement we get from the loved ones and the ones who claim to love us across the deep. The whole cry now is over there "Go get 'em boys and hurry back home; everything will be yours on your return. We want to welcome you all victors and not victims. So win the war."

That sort of word is mighty nice and it encourages us to considerable extent. But we feel sort of crushed to think they expect that we want everything to be ours when we return. It is our duty to fight and protect our country. We owe it. We only want what is coming to us in the way of courtesy, jobs, etc. This is just the way I felt about it at the time I am supposed to be writing. In the last chapter you will learn how I feel about it thirteen years after the war, the actual time I am writing this book.

As I Saw It in the Trenches

The coming of daybreak does not find us going over as we were told we would. We still lie crouched in the mud. I wish we had gone over. I want to get through with it all. Now we have to lie here to be picked on all day by machine-guns and bombs. The boy was right when he said, "It's Hell on the front." The day passes. Night passes while my mind is becoming poisoned with bitterness. The machine-guns will not let us stick our heads out of our dugouts. Bullets will sink deep into our brains if we do. The last mouthful of corn willie has long been digested or consumed with the teeth of diarrhea and dysentery. Our stomachs stink with these common trench diseases. Our clothes do not smell so good, either. Our bodies do not smell as we would like for the reason that a bath is almost impossible. A shell hole bath or spring bath is the best we can look for and nine times out of ten the men refrain from taking that sort of bath. I almost starve for something to eat. I am not thirsty any of the time for the reason that I cannot excite my sense of thirst with food and for the reason that my body seeps up water from the mud. The machine-guns keep too close vigil. We cannot stir lest we fail to stir any more. Two days and nights pass and we still lie in our dugouts still hungry and unable to get any food. My pocket mirror reveals that my eyes have taken hiding in the back of my head. Compared with the 185 pounds I brought to the front, I now won't weigh over 135 or 40 pounds.

The second night, we sneak out of our dugouts and hobble on up to the front line trenches. I almost swerve I am so weak. Before the coming of day, we sit snugged away in the lousy trench preparatory to launching an attack upon the enemy when it gets light enough. I feel that I would be a poor match for any German across no-man's land.

When the least bit of daylight creeps into the trench, men can be seen scribbling upon a little paper of some sort. They are writing home. They tell of their sad state from soon going over the top. Some of them drop tears upon the paper as they write. They know they are facing certain death. One boy scribbles the following line: "I am killed in action today. Please do not worry about me." He sniffs and cries. He knows that soon his body might be lain to rot out there. He takes out his sweetheart's photo and wets it with tears. He puts the photo back into his pocket and says, "Even though you can't, your picture is here to be buried with me."

I procure a piece of paper from this fellow and placing it upon the flat part of my rifle stock, write "Please do not worry about me just because I was killed up here today. Good-bye." We know these letters will be sent home if we are killed; otherwise, they won't be.

Broad open daylight finds us humped below the surface with a heavy blanket of fog hanging over us. The cloud almost hides us from one another. If not for the fog, we would have already been on the move. The platoon commander draws us out of the trench and makes a little talk in which he stresses the necessity of winning the war. He points out that the Germans brought it on us and that we should settle it by beating the dickens out of them. I hang my head and nod. I almost want to grit my teeth and curse in response to these remarks. We should know we are going to try to kill them to save ourselves whether we figure we are fighting for the right reason or not. I picture the squatting Germans over there waiting for us to poke our heads from a dugout or trench when the fog is gone. "Get back in your trenches," the loyal officer says.

As soon as the fog lifts we will trounce upon them. How can I with nothing but rotten entrails in my body? The kitchen force tried all night to get food to us but could not for the barrage the enemy machine-guns were laying down. The American and French artillery are tearing them to pieces. The earth again roars with thundering cannon and bursting shells. Machine-guns cackle and bullets zip over the trench top. It will be too bad when we do go over.

The fog grows less dense. It is rising. A few minutes later and we stand perched upon the parapet. Bullets whistle thick. Men have already begun to drop. They are screaming in agony. We go forward. Shells flash with challenging ire. A fellow receives a shrapnel bullet in his side and wobbles back into the trench. The bullets whistle so thick that I duck my head and pull my helmet over my left ear so the bullets whistle mostly from our left front.

The Americans charge fast across no-man's land. I expect Germans any time. I expect to see their heads and shoulders above a trench any moment. I expect to see bayonets flip out first followed by the grey uniforms. A squad of Germans come running across a knoll with hands up.

They jump through a small mass of barbed wire and continue towards us saying and yelling "Kamerad." They continue to the rear. A few minutes later a hundred or more Germans jump from a trench with hands hoisted into the air. This looks fine and if not for the enemy machine-guns and artillery fire, we could smile from unloading suspense.

My helmet flounces upon my head when a shrapnel or fragment glances it. I fall to my knees and then jump into a large shell hole for a few seconds. I look to my left and in a shell hole a big German lies with head supported in his hand. Blood flows from his face as he tries to display friendliness by disturbing the blood on his face with a smile and shaking his head as though to mean that it is a tough situation for both him and me. I jump up and walk on a short distance. I hear the German screaming and chattering in his language. I look around quickly and discover that an American corporal is walking toward him holding his rifle in readiness to shoot the wounded German. The German begs hysterically for his life. The American throws the safety and brings the rifle to his shoulder. The wounded man throws his hands over his face. I yell at the corporal not to shoot the wounded enemy. The rifle flashes. A bullet pierces the victim's hands; they drop from his face and blood begins to ooze from a small hole over the dying German's left eye.

The corporal walks up to me and says, "You must be a Germany sympathizer."

"It looks like it, doesn't it? I am half dead from being exposed to their weapons and still am fighting them; fighting those who have guns in their arms and hands ready to shoot my head off; but not fighting those who have lain down their arms from being wounded." I reply.

The corporal walks on. "Maybe I shouldn't have said that," I think. But still I cannot see wherein it is right to shoot a wounded prisoner.

A lieutenant falls in front of me. He dies almost instantly. While I gaze at the officer who trembles from dying, a man punches me and says, "They almost got you, didn't they?"

"Yes! And I guess they will yet," I reply. I do not understand the meaning of his question until he says, "The oil has leaked out all over your pants and leggings."

Searching myself for the oil he mentioned about, I find that a bullet has passed through my rifle stock, puncturing the oil can and tearing a splinter off the stock.

28. In Hell Again

Before going very much further, I feel a jar on my heel and looking down discover that a bullet has passed all the way through my left shoe heel. The explosion of a shell nearby finds me lying flat on the ground and trembling as clots of dirt rain down upon me. A slow drizzly rain causes mud to collect on our shoes as we walk along. When the collection on our feet get too heavy, it all flakes off and our feet feel as light as a dime.

Coming on top of a hill at almost the end of our objective, the captain yells, "While we have them on the run, let's keep them on the run."

The captain discovering a town some distance away, says, "We must sleep in that town tonight. Let's don't let them stop."

Fleeing Germans can be seen running toward the town. They are too far away to shoot, however. Germans can be seen across the valley on the next hill feeding their cannon. Shells burst thick around us all the time. Shrapnel race through the air seemingly trying to best one another to the prey.

The fleeing Germans run to our left. They seem to be trying to evade being captured. I must be one of the first to see that for when I fall to my belly and begin shooting, others take up the fire and soon the two enemies are lying down. When I first take up the fire, I shoot at the man in the lead. He falls and by that time the other man is being fired upon and then he falls. By the time I get ready to record this addition on my rifle, my German jumps up and begins running again. I fire upon him again until someone almost lays his rifle barrel upon my head and shoots. The sharp concussion nearly cracks my eardrums and I bring down my first oath in days. I can look back to take up fire again and by this time my German has overtaken the other. The latter then jumps up and they both run right off before our eyes while our rifles bark at them vociferously. They disappear instantly as if being swallowed up by the earth to save them from being killed. I suppose they jumped in a trench and escaped by the way of it.

A few minutes later a runner-boy runs up to the captain and hands him a note. The commander quickly reading says, "We must wait here for we have driven a wedge in the lines."

In response to his command, every man hunts a hole to shield himself from the bullets. The shell hole I occupy is not so large, and occasionally bullets pick up the ground right in my face. I do not like this and crouch as low as I can. I jerk my muscles as they zip so close over. The gun changing its range, I look up in response to seeking a larger hole and find that Captain Woodside has been shot down. He lies in a small hole frowning from the bullets he has received in his hip. I feel sorry for the brave and faithful captain and feel lost also.

Another covey of bullets puts me in the bottom of my shell hole until they have flown well by. I again come quickly to surface and sighting a large dugout in front, adjust my muscles preparatory to bouncing into it. I am attracted by three men that lie crouching in the hole. Fearing that I will be unwelcome and that the earthly abode will be too crowded besides, I withhold my intentions and look in another direction. While I am held between two or three intentions, a shell lights in the shell hole in front blowing the men all to pieces. Dirt stings my face and had it not been for the walls of the hole, the chances are a hundred to one I would have been killed instantly. A few minutes later an officer jumps up, blows a whistle and motions the men to the rear. This means that something is wrong that I know nothing about. All that can walk get on the go and run followed by as many machine-gun bullets as I ever heard whistle by. While I do not have much strength, I put all I have into the race. The mud that collects on my feet in the run, fleeks off when it becomes too heavy and then it seems that I can outrun a horse. Men running fast when shot down almost turn flips.

We do not retreat more than fifty yards until we are stopped by a sergeant who yells madly at the men not to run any further. He screams "We must hold them. We cannot retreat any further."

On stopping, everyone shoots back in the direction of the enemy whether he sees anything or not. I learn that we were about to be surrounded by the enemy who slipped up close by the use of trenches.

Discovering that the Company barber is badly hurt, I turn over several times and stop by him. "What is the matter?" I ask. The barber fails to answer. His lips are as white as cotton almost. He tries to support himself but flops back. By this time I notice that his left arm is very bloody. Cutting his sleeve off, I find that he has five bullet holes in his arm. His arm is a solid red. I jerk his handkerchief from his pocket and wipe the blood away as best I can. Applying first aid until all his is used up, I push him over on his right side to await the decision of Providence. Thus, I pay the price of my haircut the only way possible in this place. Before leaving the barber, I find that he has a bullet hole in his neck. The wound does not bleed much and on examining, I find that the bullet only pierces his neck a little beyond the skin. The force of the bullet must have been almost spent by the time it reached the barber.

I look for the enemy to trounce upon us any time but they do not show themselves over the hilltop. I feel terribly shaky since losing the leadership of the captain and the loss of so many men. The Company is looking mighty slim by now since most of it has been left upon the territory we have covered. The falling of more shells than usual entices me to seek more inviting safety since the fear that the enemy intends to attack has left me.

29

Caught Napping

Our anti-aircraft guns are banging at enemy planes above us. The planes roar as they try to flee away from the barrage of clacking bombs. I have already slid into a shallow shell hole. The earth seems mad with spouting geysers and rattling machine-guns. Fragments from the shells spent in the air through effort to bring the enemy planes down, occasionally can be heard buzzing and falling upon the ground nearby. While I lie trembling and jerking from today's experiences, I hear a large fragment buzzing directly over me. By the time I twitch preparatory to crouching more constrictingly, a piece of steel falls upon my leg about midway between my knee and ankle. It strikes my leg with the oval side; otherwise it might have chopped a severe wound out of my limb. My leg burns almost as if so much fire had fallen upon it, crippling me for three weeks after this happens; and today, thirteen years later, I have no hair on the place where I was hit by the fragment.

It seems that there is more shelling right at this point than any other place nearby. Hence, I make up my mind to seek a place of less intensity and a larger shell hole. It has been my custom all the time to evade heavy points of shell fire, especially while advancing. Jumping from my shell hole I crawl as fast as possible down the hill for a distance of about twenty yards. Farther down, I discover the end of a trench and about this time bullets begin kicking up dirt nearby.

Shells have fallen so much that I can hardly hear one coming. My ears ring as if bells are inside of my head. The German artillery seems to function well and many an American has gone down already from its effect. A lieutenant walks along bleeding profusely above the left ankle. He seems to have a lot of courage and will not give up the advance. Awhile later, I pass him lying in a shell hole unable to continue any further. He is bandaging his wound which reveals that he has been hit by two machine-gun bullets.

Apparently half the men in the Company are killed and wounded by now. The ground is covered with them but one cannot realize how many lie wounded and dead upon the ground until he looks back over the surface in the rear. The air has for some time carried the cries of those badly wounded. A guy with one of his fingers skinned a little runs up to me and says, "Do you reckon I am wounded bad enough to go to the hospital?"

I say, "Yes, beat it back down the hill or you will die." He runs back with the swiftness of a sprinter. I am sure a million dollars could not buy his wound.

Discovering a pack on a dead man that has a box of hard tack in it, I remove it from the body and become its possessor. I throw my old torn pack away because it is almost ruined and for the reason that my mess-kit is so badly damaged. I jump up and soon lie sprawled in the trench while the bullets continue to zip above its top.

My wind being so short as a result of so much loss of sleep and nothing to eat, I breathe heavily. Just before ducking into the trench, I discover a dead German upon the parapet. Hoping that the body might have something to eat on it, I ease up to where it is, reaching my hand over the parapet, and grasping the foot to pull it into the trench. I never once think but that the German was killed today. Giving a quick jerk, I feel his foot slip loose from his ankle. The rotten odor from the body fans my face and I almost tear my stomach loose.

A little further down the trench, it is at least a foot deeper and curves sharply. I take up temporary abode in the curve and listen to the bombs falling out there while bullets zip over and planes hover low down for some purpose or other. The men in the planes remind me of sea divers with their goggles peeking over the sides of the planes. It seems that everything is out for the kill today, as usual, and that every time I make a move for my own advantage my efforts are immediately mocked by some trick the enemy pulls on me. I am extremely weak and my belly is as flabby and empty as a punctured inner tube. I cannot say that I am so hungry. Diarrhea takes care of my appetite. I can hold my eyes open only when a shell showers me with dirt. I am so physically disabled that should the enemy challenge us for a hand-to-hand engagement, they would gore through-and-through my empty hollow with my inability to offer hardly any resistance.

As I lie recalling the past, my eyes heavily close. I am half asleep. My inactive mind recalls the horrors of this cruel day, for I can see men running to gore one another to death. I can see the men sweat under the heavy loads of mud on their feet. I can see the German with out-stretched hands pleading for his life. I can see his wife and babies drop-ping tears upon a telegram they receive relative to his death. I can see khaki uniforms falling and rolling upon the ground begging and crying for someone to help them. I seem to have lost most of my fear for the outcome of the vociferous threat out there. I am soon snatched into slumber to begin dreaming of it all.

I can hear the bombs banging away and the planes roaring over even though I sleep and ignore their roaring and banging madness. If a bomb should end it all, it is no more than I could expect and too, it would all amount to so little should one catch me napping. I sleep on while the shells occasionally jar the earth about me. I can hear the splinters and shrapnel pass harmlessly over the trench. I can hear wounded crying in the distance. I sleep on and some time later, I do not know how much later, I can feel something knocking on the sole of my hob-nails. I have become accustomed to threats and jars. They are now only matter of fact occurrences. Why should I awake and jump running from the trench just because something tries to disturb me by tapping on my shoe? I should not have unless the origin of the dis-turbance turns me a somersault. I should worry and it all merely turns out to be a peaceful dream for the time being. I can imagine someone tapping my foot to wake me up for dinner or something else good. I for-get in my sleep that I lie in a lousy den subject to being blown into its walls. I forget that we are in the middle of banging hell dodging the torches the many demons sling at us. No doubt I can be heard snoring among the bang of the shells. The longer I sleep the more removed my mind gets from the throat-slashing incidents that keep vigil over us. The fact that I am sleeping does not mean that my mind is at perfect rest. It continues to picture before me the good and bad experiences of life. I imagine in my dream that I am stretched out under a cool tree far removed from hostilities that entertain the thousands of cootie carriers in this torn and bullet-picked country. I can yet hear the bang of the shells but I am accustomed to such reports and I do not intend to let them worry me. I now hear someone dying from a shell or something that got him, maybe while his mind was divided among thoughts. It is a German who cries and calls for someone while the knives of death strive to put an end to the beat of his heart. The voice comes from the rear. It seems that the dying victim is on the parapet just above me. I sleep on and good fate, if such has ever visited this place, seems to see to it that all such sad and cruel incidents shall not disturb my few minutes of rest. I sleep, dream and hear things all at the same time. My deep slumber drives my natural care for unpleasant voices, cries, and deathly reports from my mind. The continuous disturbance at the other end of my body does not worry me. What if something is beating on my foot? That is all right so long as my foot is not jerked from my ankle. What if we have driven a wedge in our lines? That is all right so long as we are in no danger of being massacred by the enemy. And if the rest of us are killed, that should be all right too. Nearly all the Company has already been killed and wounded. We are no better than they are. The captain now lies wounded in no-man's land—the land that not many minutes ago was ours through conquest. If he is meant to give his hip or life to this cause, be it a just or unjust one, we should be willing to give something for it.

Now the thumps upon my foot shake my whole body. I can feel myself shake upon my back. I can feel my pack move under my body. I can feel my rifle move across my belly for it is there that I place the barrel in order that I can grab it in response to protection from any unwelcome intruder. I am not aware that probably something that would rather kill me than let me live holds my principal defense: my rifle. I yet have my bayonet but what is a little old bayonet without a rifle on which to use it? I am not aware that probably I am being looked upon by people who prefer that I realize that I am facing my fatal doom to killing me while I know nothing of it and robbing them of their kick of seeing me beg at their feet for my life. Even though I sleep, I feel something nudging about my neck. I am not aware that probably something is taking the last bite I have been lucky enough to get hold of for over two days and nights. I am dead to the knowledge of any of it. I am too deeply absorbed in sleep to really know just what is taking place. I feel it and hear nearly all of it but I hold on to my period of rest at the cost of being stripped naked and maybe of being killed should my intruder see fit.

The feeling that something of detrimental disturbance has taken up abode with me comes over me for the first time when I am shaken severely from foot to head. It is then that I feel that all the time something might have been going wrong. It is then that I become far less hovered with the weight of sleep. It is now that I can hear the dying enemy gently repeating two words that sound like he says, "Mutter Jane." I know now that something is going wrong. I realize that I am caught napping. I realize that poor strategy results in something bad for me. I know that my rifle is taken from me for I felt it leaving my person while I slept. My blood runs fast and cold. I blare my eyes open as I quickly come to my haunches. Three figures sit humped in front of me. I shake my head through trying to adjust my eyes to the light since I have slept with my face in darkness underneath my helmet. They kick me again for they are in a hurry to get going. I fully realize now that I am helpless at the hand of five Germans, there being two more squatted to my right that I had not noticed when I discovered the first three. Their faces display contempt but probably they are not as angry as they look. Being in a hurry to take me back, it might be that the Germans look the part in order to get me to act quickly. The man heading the trio punches me with the butt of his rifle, mutters something and motions me down the trench. The first man to my right reaches over my shoulder and relieves me of my box of hard tack. Dropping my helmet while gaining my feet, the first man of the three picks it up and places it on my head almost as comfortably as I could have placed it myself. Getting on the move, I am followed by three Germans and I follow two of them. Fearing that my own men will see my hands above the trench top, the man behind me again bumps me with his rifle and looking around at him he motions me to get lower. I obey promptly and before going many feet, my legs begin aching and weakening from walking in such an uncomfortable position. The enemy in front carries my rifle a little way and then pitches it over the trench top. The dying German's voice fades away as we increase the distance between him and us.

Moving about fifty yards down the trench, my captors motion me outside; for at this point the trench is shallower and we are not in great danger of being seen by the Americans. My mind has taken up an entirely different line of thought by now. Many ideas and imaginations come to me. One of my first thoughts is, had I rather be a prisoner of the Germans somewhere back of the mad hostilities or fighting on the front with my own men who are every minute exposed to certain death for somebody. I can imagine myself pinned up in a lousy German prison camp, being fed just enough to keep alive on. On the other hand, I can see myself crouched down in a shell hole or dugout exposed to mad barrages or advancing against a hundred machine-guns that mow men down like cats. I can imagine my captors or some other mean Germans slapping me through trying to force me to tell certain details relative to the American forces. I recall the many stories that have been told about the cruelty the enemy administers to the prisoners. I have been told that they cut off the ears of men sometimes, that they jab their eyes out, etc. However, I have never believed much of this and I do not become very excited at these recollections. All these thoughts flash through my mind in one-hundredth less time than it takes to tell it.

Getting out of the trench, I find that the surface nearby is covered with shallow dugouts. Several of them contain Germans, most of whom smoke. They do not seem at all stirred at my being one of their prisoners. They puff away on their cigarettes as though they are back in Germany taking a week off from their work.

Back up on the hill among my own men shells still pour down sending dirt and smoke into the air. By now, I am trying to make up my mind that Providence directs my being taken captive. Probably all this means the sparing of me from this war alive. Eating a good old can of chicken soup with a few of my grey friends would indeed be a welcomed little feast. I am no longer so very excited for I realize that whatever happens, it cannot be much worse than my experiences so far at the front. But miracles do work up here every day and I suppose one is beginning its maneuvers now, for I hear something swishing through the air. I look around and see a large flare shooting into the air. The

Germans seem excited and stop. They look with curiosity at the signals. We all know the Americans are signaling for something. The Germans squat down and I follow. They mumble to one another and glance at me in the meantime. "Ah!" I think. "Guess they will attend to me in the event anything turns up."

I really will not be surprised if a gun is pointed at me and relieves me of all the misery at the front. My heart begins to flutter. I should not like to die quite yet as I thought I might back there in the trench.

The Germans begin scattering. I sit still for yet I cannot hear the approach of shell unless they are almost upon me. Now I hear them. They are banging upon the ground almost among us. I jump to my feet and soon roll head foremost into a fairly large dugout. By the time I crouch as low as possible, something heavy bumps me with the force of a football tackle. Quickly looking up, I find that a big German is sharing the small hole with me. His face resting almost against mine, I can smell the odor of cigarettes on his breath. Craving a smoke immensely, I say, "Give me a cigarette." He does not respond and so I try no further to bum him of one of his cigarettes. Of course, I do not suppose he understands me in the first place and besides, I suppose he thinks this is no place to carry on a conversation.

The barrage lasts for a minute or two and lifts. I hear the voices of people and looking up find that the Americans are launching a counterattack. The Germans seem to make no effort towards defense but instead jump from their dugouts with hands up. The German beside me jumps from the dugout and gives himself up and then I follow and soon pass the prisoners that are being searched by the Americans. All the men are not across the trench yet. I jump the trench and run up the side of it a little way until I find a dead man from whose body I procure a rifle. The shelling has about all stopped and the prisoners are on the move to the rear.

The excitement decreasing, I walk up to a fellow and ask him for a cigarette. The man is very kind and having cigarettes pulls out his package and says, "Help yourself."

He takes one himself and lights it. Handing me his box of matches, I remove one from the box and proceed to strike it on the box. Before it lights, the man falls to the ground and hearing bullets zipping by, I jump in a shell hole until the barrage passes by. Quickly looking up then, I find that a bullet struck him in the temple, killing him instantly. Relieving him of his tin of beef, I eat for the first time in more than two days. I do not feel so hungry and therefore do not eat much. Smoking the cigarette after eating seems to give me more pep than the food.

30

Growing More and More Disgusted

It is well known that we have taken our objective and I do not doubt but we have a little more than done that. It is a terrible thing to do. It is enough to cause a fellow to go mad and run away. I am becoming more and more disgusted. One might think I have little to feel that way about since we have been extremely victorious so far as conquest is concerned. That is all right, but a string of victories can finally end one becoming disgusted if every time he goes over, there are as many Germans as ever. And too, one gets tired from having to go over so many times. We think that probably the last battle will result in our getting a good rest removed from the banging shell and clattering machine-guns. Before we realize it is our time to return and go over again, we are told to roll pack and move up to the front.

I know I have much to be thankful for all right. The men left in the Company today could be carried away in a one-horse wagon. It is easy to tell that the Company has suffered an amazing number of deaths and casualties. I am thankful to be left still afoot. Every commissioned officer has either been killed or wounded today. Only a corporal or two is left to direct the remnant of the Company should the Germans attack.

A man walks down the hill towards us. He has his breeches stripped to his knees which reveals that his crotch is extremely bloody. Coming nearer, I find that he is hit by bullet or fragment in the stride and that one of his testicles hangs unprotected.

A fellow whose name is Levy passes nearby me. He carries an ugly wound about his face. Knowing that he is a sort of peculiar fellow, I ask,

"Is that the best you can do to come up here on this front and get all shot up?"

In reply, he says, "And you are liable to get your damned head shot off before the sun goes down."

Darkness finds most of us on our feet digging-in. I only deepen my shell hole a little to be sure that I am not exposed to the flying bullets. Awhile after retiring, I hear a shell coming and pull every muscle in my body into a knot through contractions. It lands nearby, killing a man instantly. I peek over the side of my dugout just as the victim falls and rolls over leaving his front to me. It not being very dark, I can see that the shell fragments struck him about the groins almost tearing his breeches off him. Things getting quieter, I crawl out to the body and return with a tin of beef. Tucking it away until tomorrow, I eat a little of what was left from the other can.

Out into the darkness, I can hear wounded carrying on. Some of them curse and swear while some of them on the other hand pray and call someone. The neck of the dead man just outside my dugout gurgles and since I am all alone in my dugout, I become a little restless. To make things more nauseating, one of our artillery-guns is falling its bombs short of range which means the shells are falling close to me. However, a signal soon results in the gun changing its range and this worry is quite over.

Daybreak. A fresh body of Americans is advancing and passing among our dugouts. The air breathes heavily with machine-gun bullets. Bombs fall also but in surprisingly less numbers than yesterday. The American infantrymen duck their heads against the swarming bullets. I know if I should look outside, I could see them falling in the event a bullet did not stick in my own head. Machine-guns can be heard barking in the distance and bombs can be heard flying over.

A half hour later the Americans have the enemy on the run leaving us out of intense danger. Perching upon my dugout, I eat some more corned beef with another young recruit that joins me. While we are partaking of the beef, several German prisoners pass by among whom is a man who looks exactly like a fellow near my home whose name is Simpson. Looking straight at him, I say, "How do you do, Mr. Simpson?"

The boy says, "Do you know him?"

"Yes," I reply. "I knew him in Germany." I almost strangle myself when I burst into a loud laugh at the idea of him being so absent-minded as to ask such a question. Thinking of what he did, he says, "Ah, hell, I ought to have known you never had seen that blamed German."

The Company retires beyond the hill to the rear in order to get out of range of machine-guns. The Company is terribly depleted. The dressing station is now located at the foot of the hill we are on. The wounded who have been taken there for attention can be heard complaining loudly. I help carry a fellow who is badly wounded down to the station. The men carry on pitifully and some of them nurse very bad wounds. I recognize some men of my own Company among the wounded. Running out of dressing apparel, I am asked to go back over the hill and bring up some more. Not having the courage to refuse, although I felt like it, I get on the move and coming to the top of the hill a one-pounder opens up on me and I feel for one of the deathly little demons to blow me into frazzles before I can make it out of its range. I run as fast as I can which is very slow at that, and then walk until I come across a deep trench into which I roll and breathe heavily for some time. When the one-pounder ceases firing and I feel that I can get on the go again, I pull out of the trench and trot, listening every second for the gun to open fire upon me again. It does not again, however, and soon I reach the station where many more wounded lie. While waiting for my chance to ask for the dressing material, a wounded German asks me for a box of hard tack I had picked up. He asks by pointing to the box and pulls out some cigarettes and offers them to me. I break the box half in two, giving him half of it and taking a few cigarettes in return. Another wounded German lying nearby refuses the other half of hard tack and seems not to be so badly hurt. Not a minute longer he jerks his whole body into contractions and passes out of this world into the next.

On my way back, I meet a red-headed young man who weeps loudly.

"What is the matter with you?" I ask.

"My twin brother just got killed," he replies.

After leaving the heartbroken fellow, I come across a red-headed dead fellow with a bullet through his head. I am certain the slain man is a brother to the man to whom I talked.

Before reaching the station, a machine-gun opens fire on me picking up dirt around my feet. I can tell by the force of the bullets the gun is a long way off. Being so disgusted with it all, I for the first time since being shot by Germans, give no heed to the bullets but really wish one would plug me in the leg or foot as I do not believe I am very liable to be hit in the body. Having received no wound, I soon reach the dressing station to find many more wounded who are in urgent need of attention. Fearing that I will be asked to do something else, I beat it up the hill to the little remnant of the Company. On reaching my dugout, I find that Harry is still alive as a result of which I am very pleased. He comes over to my dugout and we talk awhile during which time I tell him just how tired and disgusted I am with it all. We are both very downhearted.

Dark finds us bunking in a small shanty a mile or so from the nearest point of machine-gun fire. We spread our blankets each on a crudely constructed wire support. Before we get to dozing, the Germans begin shelling the swamp, which entices us to get outside and dig-in. Digging-in just behind the shanty, we lie down and talk until the shelling ceases. Daylight finds us back in the shanty snoring away. Harry wakes up first and gets on the hunt for something to eat. He becomes vexed because I won't get up and help him and literally bawls me out. He blares his eyes at me and tells me just how lazy I am. Discovering my chance to tease him, I stretch my hands back over my head and say, "Ain't it nice to have someone to get out and hunt for something to eat for him while he lies up and sleeps?" At this remark, he gets back by saying, "The hell with you. You can go to hell from now on."

Before Harry knows it, I am up and on the hunt myself. Discovering a Company of men getting their ration across a field from where

Page missing.

yesterday's engagements. I could have sympathized for the captain more had not the bullets been hissing around me the same time he went down under a fusillade of them.

I carry the opinion that the Company barber is left to rot where I left him. My friend Bockleman is missing and through inquiry I learn that he was either killed or taken captive yesterday. I saw Clift at the dressing station yesterday afternoon when I went back for first aid material. He carries two wounds in his left leg.

By noon we are digging-in on an open hill about two miles from the front at a different point than yesterday. I am awfully knocked out and feel just like I imagine an old knocked-out ox feels after working under heavy strain for years. So feeling that I care not to dig a whole dugout, I call another fellow whose dugout buddy has been killed and propose to him to dig-in with me. He agrees and within a half hour's time, we have our dugout quite finished. Before finishing, however, I realize that I am sunk when I get a whiff of his body. He out-stinks any man at the front dead or alive but being a fellow who always tries to stick to a bargain, I put in to live through if possible. The results of his diarrhea spreads all over him and I might exaggerate just a little when I say that a dead body smells pleasantly compared with his. The gasses that cut-up in his belly just won't stay inside and it is only through the aid of my gas mask that I am able to stick it out through the night. Another fellow who strolls in during the night finds me sitting outside the dugout and asks if he can dugout with me being that he is tired and sleepy and does not feel like digging-in. Assuring him that it is quite all right with me, he crawls inside but soon crawls back out saying, "God——! I don't wonder at your not staying in there."

At daylight, we both lie outside lying on our blankets and covering with our overcoats. The coming of a big frost whitens our legs from knees down and my feet feel like they had taken quarters in a refrigerator. We build a fire, warm good and walk down to the banks of a deep brooklet to get our share of the ham of a dead mule recently killed by a high explosive. While we are very hungry all right, my companion and I cook a little of it just to have it to say we ate a piece of mule. The meat being so coarse and the idea of it being mule, I refuse to swallow mine at first. But being determined to eat some of it if my partner could, I finally swallowed some and kept it down by placing a tin of beef on top of it.

Three days later we yet have no recruits. Only the remaining twenty-eight men still compose the Company. We are moved to a wooded sector of the front at night and take up lousy dugouts among trees and bushes. The dugouts are covered with sheet iron and would be comfortable for dugouts if they were not so exposed to shellfire and alive with cooties. It is a big job to keep the cooties off one's body and as a result my arms above the elbows are bloody from being eaten on by the nasty little creatures. I try every way possible to exterminate them but so many of them take hiding in the woolen underwear that it is impossible to get rid of many of them at the time. In addition, a new supply delivers themselves to me most every day.

The second night we are here, Cox suffers the loss of one of his legs that is chopped off by a dud that falls into his dugout while he sleeps. He is taken from his dugout screaming and crying and I do not know until morning that it is he that is wounded. Today is Saturday. I remark that I am going to shave and look spry as tomorrow is Sunday. A fellow says, "I don't know what there is up here to look spry for; it will be a good long time until we have anything to look spry for."

A guy who hears him and who has his breeches nearly torn off by wire entanglement, says, "As sure as I am without a pair of breeches I'll bet you we eat dinner at home Christmas."

"Gee!" I exclaim, "How crazy you are, man, to talk that way. We couldn't eat dinner at home Christmas if we should be discharged right now."

The man contends that he knows what he is talking about and challenges anyone to bet on it. I listen on while I try with partial success to lather my beardy face with some of the white soap we use at the front. I shave by cutting three or four off at a time with my safety razor. Spending at least an hour on my face, I finally get them off with the exception of the healthy growth under my nose. After coming out of my dugout, I hear someone say, "That must be a new recruit."

I look at him and say, "No, not quite a new recruit; just a new shave."

He says, "Now get a new haircut and you will be all dolled-up.

I reply, "If you will do the cutting I will furnish the hair."

Sunday finds me all by myself perched in a dugout on the top of a high hill looking for any curiously-behaving Germans. At first, I get somewhat a kick out of spying upon the enemy with the field glasses furnished me. I can easily see the enemy lorries rolling far in the distance. I can see the drivers sitting upon the wagons jerking the lines fastened to the horses. I can see a few scattering towns far away where the enemy resides. But this only entertains me for awhile. The day becomes more lonesome than any day I ever previously experienced. Everything is still. I cannot even hear a bird whistle or sing out here on this God-forsaken hill. I cannot hear anyone talk and only occasionally I can hear a gun shoot far in the distance. I begin recalling the past and begin seeing so many things that happened on the front that I always swore I should try to keep out of my memory. I can see the blood pouring from dying men as they beg for something to comfort them in their dying moments. Red's and my friend Easterday's bodies are rotten by now. My best pal Harry is in the hospital unless he is dead from the gas he got. I have had bad breaks all through it; and I have had good breaks too. If I could ever leave this stinking front to never again return, it would be too good to be true. I would not go through with it all again for a million dollars if I could have my way about it. It is all too ridiculous for any-thing. I never hated anything half like I hate all this mess up here. We are here getting killed and spending the best part of our youth killing and being killed by these Germans. They probably think they are fighting for that which they think to be just and I do not know if I am or not. This could as easily be a political war sponsored by those birds who are sending us word to go ahead and win the war. I have my doubts that some of them want it to end so long as it means big money in connection with their interests.

I recall the good old Sundays I have spent at my home in the coun-try quite removed from the fast American life. The good old Sundays spent at the old country church talking with all the neighbors is easily recalled. I can recall the athletic events I always loved so much and the boys that engaged in them with me. Everything so seen is pictured as awfully enjoyable compared with the hell up here that strives to pull everyone in at its door. I cannot foresee those good old times any more. The war seems too far from the end to entertain the thought of ever returning and resuming those used-to-be good times. We did not appre-ciate all the good things of life while we were having them. It is now while we face and fight back everything that tries to take our lives that we come to enjoy the things we were too inexperienced to enjoy, a lesson for those who are lucky enough to come through it all alive to say noth-ing of being whole.

While my mind searches the past and strives to drive the mad thoughts from my mind by the beautiful recollections, my throat swells and chokes. My heart becomes too heavy. I close my eyes to try and close my memory to the world that I hate and that so seems to hate me. I close my eyes to the darn shell holes and pulverized dirt that have been my view for the last four months. I do it all through effort to drive those hateful memories from my mind in order that I might be able to refresh it with the sweet memories that painted my career before I ever heard a shell or machine-gun speak. I open my eyes to find that everything is a blur before me. My eyes run wet as a result of the sweet and past recollections. I am the most lonesome man in the world as I sit on this hilltop imagining that I have not a friend this side of the Atlantic.

My feet have been throbbing for some time. They not only throb; now they really hurt. I remove my shoes through effort to ease them but this action does no good. I warm them and that does no good. Nothing helps that I do. I cannot understand it at all. My feet were always strong and gave me no trouble.

By night, I am back in my dugout nursing painful feet. I am beginning to believe I have been in the trenches just long enough to bring it all on myself.

A shell comes over and takes the lives of two off with it. Good is this as we bury them when daylight comes. We spread a blanket over them and their faces and pitch a little dirt over them, not covering their feet. A chaplain who has come up to the front holds a short prayer and then they are left to rot like the rest of the dead up here. I am unaware that these two men are the last that I see buried at the front.

Late in the afternoon, we are relieved and I am told are going back for a little rest and to re-mobilize the Company. By the time we are two miles from the front, my feet become too painful to proceed with the Company and hence, I fall out. I can tell by tire tracks that ambulances come close to the front at night for wounded soldiers. Therefore, I make up my mind to wait until one comes along or until I am able to get help from some source or other. Late in the night I hear an ambulance coming up the road. The machine moves slowly as it is too dark to undertake speeding-up. Coming near me, I holler at the driver and inquire if I can get a place on his machine so that I can get back to the infirmary or dressing station. He points down the hill and shows me a dim light that burns inside a tent. He tells me to go there and get dressed and that he will be back by there in an hour or two to pick up men ready to be dispatched to the hospital. Extremely glad of the information, I pull out for the dressing station and soon find that I am terribly tangled up in barbed wire entanglement. I work at least an hour before I am free and entering the station. The doctors and orderlies laugh at my clothes being picked up so badly by the wire and tell me that I undoubtedly have gotten in the range of a machine-gun.

"Not lately," I reply.

They soon have me dressed, lying by a warm stove and waiting for the ambulance. They worry me a great deal by asking about when the 3rd Division is leaving the front. I tell them I know no more than they know. I beg them for my helmet since it has my name and two bullet marks carved upon it. They please me by letting me carry it with me.

A large shell falls too close by to make things comfortable. I live under suspense until the ambulance comes. An hour or two after getting dressed, the ambulance brings more wounded and takes out those of us who are dressed and ready for transportation. One man is shot up terribly and screams and yells as if to be dying. The road is rough and rendering the ambulance very rough and uncomfortable. The heavy shelling continues close and that adds to the unpleasantness. The badly-wounded man says he must stop and answer a natural calling. "What is it you want to do?" I ask him.

"I want to wet," he replies.

Taking no chances on getting blown to death by the big monster that bellows through so often, I agree for him to use my highly-prized helmet in order that he will not hold up the ambulance.

Index

Index